# Bouquet & the
# Ohio Indian War

# Bouquet & the Ohio Indian War
## Two Accounts of the Campaigns of 1763-1764

### Bouquet's Campaigns
Cyrus Cort

### The History of Bouquet's Expeditions
William Smith

*Bouquet & the Ohio Indian War:*
*Two Accounts of the Campaigns of 1763-1764*
*Bouquet's Campaigns*
by Cyrus Cort
*The History of Bouquet's Expeditions*
by William Smith


First published under the titles
*Bouquet's Campaigns*
and
*The History of Bouquet's Expeditions*


Leonaur is an imprint of Oakpast Ltd

Copyright in this form © 2018 Oakpast Ltd


ISBN: 978-1-84677-584-0 (hardcover)
ISBN: 978-1-84677-583-3 (softcover)

http://www.leonaur.com


Publisher's Notes

The opinions of the authors represent a view of events in which he was a participant related from his own perspective, as such the text is relevant as an historical document.

The views expressed in this book are not necessarily those of the publisher.

# Contents

Bouquet's Campaigns     7

The History of Bouquet's Expeditions     145

# Bouquet's Campaigns

HENRY BOUQUET

# Contents

| | |
|---|---|
| Introduction | 13 |
| Bouquet's Birthplace | 17 |
| Bouquet Leaves Home | 20 |
| How Bouquet Spent Leisure Time | 22 |
| Enters British Service Royal Americans | 23 |
| Bouquet goes to Philadelphia | 25 |
| Forbes' Expedition and Dispute with Washington | 27 |
| Bouquet in Command | 34 |
| Byerly at Bushy Run | 35 |
| Pontiac's Conspiracy | 37 |
| Siege of Detroit | 40 |
| Siege of Fort Pitt and Ligonier | 42 |
| The Flight of the Byerlys to Fort Ligonier | 45 |
| Defence of Fort Ligonier | 50 |
| The Situation at Carlisle | 54 |
| The March to Bedford | 58 |
| The March to Ligonier | 60 |
| Bouquet's Army of Deliverance | 61 |

| | |
|---|---|
| Bushy Run Battle | 62 |
| Report of the First Day's Fight Near Bushy Run | 65 |
| Second Day's Fight, August 6 | 69 |
| Bouquets' Report of Second Day's Fight | 74 |
| The Ownership of the Bushy Run Tract | 81 |
| Evil Results of Provincial Apathy | 85 |
| Massacre of a Schoolmaster and Ten Scholars | 89 |
| Campaign of 1764 | 92 |
| Desertions of Provincial Troops | 94 |
| Arrival at Fort Pitt | 96 |
| The March into Ohio | 97 |
| Council on the Muskingum—Captives Restored | 99 |
| Public Thanks to Bouquet | 108 |
| Injustice and Ingratitude of Virginia | 109 |
| Bouquet's Promotion | 111 |
| Leaves for Pensacola Will and Death | 113 |
| Bouquet's Grave Unknown | 117 |
| Bouquet's Grave | 120 |
| A Monument Due Bouquet | 122 |
| Concluding Remarks | 125 |
| Pontiac's Submission | 126 |
| Pontiac's Assassination and its Expiation | 128 |
| Westmoreland County Before and During the Revolution | 133 |
| Attack on Hannastown | 139 |
| Religious Characteristics of Early Settlers | 140 |
| Addenda | 143 |

To the precious memory of Beatrice Byerly, who escaped Pontiac's confederates and bore her tender babes through the wilderness from Bushy Run to Fort Ligonier, in 1763; who organised and conducted a Sunday school at Fort Walthour, in Westmoreland County, Pennsylvania, during the dark and dangerous days of the revolution, and who was a blessing to hundreds of pioneer settlers by her deeds of Christian charity and patriotic devotion during a long and eventful life on the frontiers, this little volume is dedicated by one of her grateful descendants.

*Though heaven alone records the tear,*
*And fame shall never know her story,*
*Her heart has shed a drop as dear*
*As e'er bedewed the field of glory.*

# Introduction

On the 26th of April 1883, a meeting was held in the arbitration room of the court house at Greensburg, Westmoreland County, Pa., to consider the propriety of celebrating the 120th anniversary of the victory of Colonel Henry Bouquet at Bushy Run, August 5 and 6, 1763, over the Confederates of Pontiac.

Ex-Lieutenant-Governor John Latta was called to the chair, and General Richard Coulter and Hon. Jacob Turney were elected Vice Presidents; Major Jas. M. Laird, Frank Vogle and Curtis Gregg were chosen as Secretaries.

By request of the meeting Rev. Cyrus Cort, a resident of Greencastle, Pa., but a native of Greensburg, Pa., was called upon to address the meeting, which he did for over half an hour, eulogizing the character and achievements of Bouquet and showing the far-reaching results of his decisive victory at Bushy Run. Rev. Cort read a letter from Hon. Joseph H. Kuhns, regretting his inability to be present and heartily approving the object of the meeting in its efforts to honour the memory of Bouquet, whose march and victory in 1763 were wonderful military achievements and did much to promote the rapid settlement of the west.

On motion, Revs. J. W. Love, W. W. Moorehead, Lucien Cort and Philip Kuhns, Dr. Kline and A. M. Sloan, Esq., were appointed a committee to draft resolutions expressive of the sense of the meeting. The following were reported:

Resolved, That in the judgement of this meeting, it is eminently right and proper to commemorate the 120th anniversary of the victory of Colonel Henry Bouquet over Pontiac's confederates at Bushy Run, August 5th and 6th, 1763.

Resolved, That inasmuch as August 5th comes on Sunday this year, and inasmuch as all the interests of humanity and Christian civilization were promoted by the decisive victory of Bouquet, we would respectfully suggest to the pastors of all of our churches in the town and county, the propriety of making such special reference to the anniversary, in their regular religious services, as in their judgement may be right and proper.

Resolved, That the victory of Bouquet be commemorated August 6th, in the grove of the old Bushy Run battlefield, by a public celebration, embracing addresses, a poem, a military display, picnic, dinner, &c.

Resolved, That a committee of arrangements, to secure and prepare the grounds; a committee on finance, to raise funds to defray necessary expenses of the celebration, and a committee to invite speakers, distinguished guests, military organizations, &c., be appointed.

The resolutions were adopted and committees in accordance appointed, as follows:

Committee of Arrangements to Secure and Prepare Grounds for the Celebration.—Amos B. Kline, J. B. Laux, Lewis Wannamaker, E. F. Houseman, Lewis Gongaware, William Moore, Mr. Shadwick, Jos. Clark, Robert Byerly, Wm. G. Shuster, Abner Cort.

Committee on Finance.—Jas. Gregg, Esq., Geo. F. Huff, Captain J. J. Wirsing, Dr. Sowash, Wm. B. Skelly, Paul Lauffer, David Snyder, John Rankin, Sebastian Baer, Esq., Hon. in. N. in Marker, H. F. Ludwick, Esq., Hon. John Hugus, and George Plumer Smith of Philadelphia.

Committee on Invitation.—General R. Coulter, Hon. Jos. H. Kuhns, Hon. Jacob Turney, Hon. John Latta, Major James M. Laird, G. D. Albert, Esq., John A. Marchand, Esq., Dr. Frank Cowan.

The annexed resolution was likewise adopted:

Resolved, That the chairmen of the three committees aforesaid be an executive committee to fill all vacancies and have a general oversight of the celebration.

A discussion then took place in regard to the advisability of issuing a pamphlet for popular circulation, giving a sketch of Colonel Bouquet and his campaigns. It was felt that such a work would form a very important factor in the celebration, and the sentiment of the meeting was that it should be issued without delay. Next day Rev. C. Cort received a letter from General Richard Coulter, A. B. Kline, Esq., and James Gregg, Esq., stating that it was the sense of the meeting that a pamphlet, consisting of one hundred pages, should be prepared as soon as possible, containing a historical sketch of Bouquet and all matters of colonial interest bearing especially on his campaign against the Confederates of Pontiac.

These gentlemen, forming the Executive Committee of the celebration, also stated further that it was their wish that he (Rev. Cort) should, prepare the aforesaid pamphlet. This task was accepted as a labour of love, with the understanding that the writer would assume all pecuniary responsibilities, and that if any profits resulted from the sale of the book or pamphlet above necessary cost of publication, the proceeds should be devoted to a fund for a monument to Bouquet

As the time was limited, and the duties of a large and laborious pastoral charge devolved upon the writer, the work has been prepared in great haste, but with conscientious care and fidelity to the facts of history and reliable traditions. I would gratefully acknowledge my obligations to writings of Francis Parkman, Geo. Harrison Fisher, C. W. Butterfield and the Penn'a Historical Society for valuable assistance in preparing this imperfect sketch of the best military man and one of the finest gentlemen and scholars of colonial times. May it help to rescue from oblivion the memory of a truly good and great man, whose heroic efforts saved our colonial ancestors from the tomahawk and scalping knife and established the supremacy of the Anglo-Saxon race in the valley of the Mississippi. Dr. Wm Smith's publication in 1765, and Dumas' sketch in 1769, form the basis of this present effort to present the facts of his life for general circulation.

At a meeting of the executive committee and committee on invitation, at which Rev. Cort was present, June 19th, it was decided to issue special invitations to the governors of Pennsylvania, Ohio and West Virginia, to the British Minister, Swiss Consul, General R. C. Drum, &c. Also, that Rev. Samuel Wilson, D.D., General James A. Beaver, Hon. W. S. Stenger and W. U. Hensel, Esq., be invited to deliver addresses at the celebration on the battlefield, Aug. 6; Dr. Frank Cowan to read a poem, and Dr. Wm. H. Egle to read a paper.

May the skies be bright and all things propitious.

# Bouquet's Birthplace

Henry Bouquet, the subject of our sketch, was born at Rolle, a small Swiss town on the northern shore of Lake Geneva in 1719. This town at that time belonged to the Canton of Berne, one of the largest and most influential Cantons of the Swiss Confederation. It now belongs to the Canton of Vaud, which is a part of French Switzerland, the dialect spoken being the Vaudois. The inhabitants since Reformation days have been chiefly members of the Reformed church, and always ardent lovers of civil and religious liberty. They are noted for industry and intelligence.

From this part of Switzerland comes a large proportion of the Swiss teachers and governesses to be met with in all parts of the world.

Lansanne, the capital of the Canton Vaud, is picturesquely situated on the southern slope of the Jura mountains and near the northern shore of Lake Geneva. It is distinguished for its religious, educational and scientific institutions. The beautiful Gothic Cathedral, begun in the 10th and completed in the 13th century, adorns the city and helps to attract vast crowds of visitors from all parts of the world. Here Gibbon, the historian resided many years, and here he wrote the greater part of his great work on the *Decline and Fall of the Roman Empire*. Here, in the western corner of Switzerland, between the Jura and the Bernese Alps, near the French borders, Henry Bouquet first saw the light. Amid the most beautiful scenery on the northern shores of the celebrated Lake Geneva which is fifty miles long and eight wide, amid orchards, vineyards and fertile farming and pasture lands, in full view of Mount Blanc and the most inspiring Alpine scenery he spent the formative days of childhood and youth. All these left their impress upon his soul and aided greatly in forming the noble and heroic character which shone forth resplendently in his future eventful career, both in the old world and the new.

Little is known of the family of Bouquet. The *Deutsche* Pioneer of Cincinnati has contended that his family name was originally Strauss from which it was changed into Bouquet, its French equivalent, when our hero had fairly begun his military career.

This is certainly a mistake founded on mere conjecture based on the analogy of such changes as Schoenberg to Belmont, &c. There is no reliable evidence to show that Bouquet ever changed his family name, much less to show that he had any special predilection for France or the French. The Vaudois people amongst whom he was born and reared have always spoken a French dialect, and in that language particularly he doubtless received his education. But it is a noteworthy fact that Bouquet always fought against France. He seemed to regard her as the representative of civil and religious despotism, and he gallantly fought against her under the banner of the government which for the time being best represented the cause and principles of constitutional liberty.

I have before me a copy of Bouquet's last Will and Testament made June 5, 1765, from which I transcribe a clause, *viz*:

> I give and bequeath to my father, if then living, or after him to Colonel Lewis Bouquet and heirs all the effects of any nature whatsoever which I may die possessed of in the Continent of Europe without exception. This would indicate that Bouquet was the original and genuine family name, and not merely the result of a capricious predilection for foreign terms. It would indicate also that the family was not so obscure as some have supposed. Mr. Konrad, the Swiss consul, has undertaken to gather data on this point which we hope will be on hand at an early day.

The war of American Independence which was looming up

at the time of Bouquet's death in 1765, and the fact that Colonel Frederick Haldimand, his executor, and to a large extent the legatee of his American possessions remained loyal to King George III. in that struggle, prevented proper examination of these matters by those most interested in Bouquet's career over a hundred years ago. This accounts in a measure also for the obscurity and comparative injustice connected with the treatment of Bouquet by writers of Colonial history.

A hundred and twenty years ago his name was a household word in America, and the memory of his heroic deeds was cherished for a generation with fond affection, by descendants of pioneer settlers whom he had rescued from the tomahawk of the red savages. Perhaps because he was a Swiss and gamed his greatest distinction in the British service on Pennsylvania soil in Colonial times the muse of history and poetry has failed to embalm and perpetuate his name and achievements in a more worthy and grateful manner.

Be this as it may, the time has come when the grateful and intelligent descendants of pioneer Colonial settlers, and all public-spirited citizens are called upon to remedy the defect and rectify the wrongs or omissions of a century, as regards the memory of one of the very best men that trod this continent before our country became a free and independent republic. To this end I have begun this narrative as an aid to the forthcoming celebration of the one hundred and twentieth anniversary of the victory of Bouquet over the confederates of Pontiac at Bushy Run, Aug. 6, 1763.

# Bouquet Leaves Home

Growing up amid the inspiring scenery of liberty loving Switzerland, Bouquet sought a theatre more commensurate with his talents and aspirations than the narrow confines bounded by his native Alps. In 1736 at the age of seventeen he made his way along the historic Rhine to the Lowlands of Holland and entered the service of the Dutch Republic, as a cadet in the Regiment of Constant.

In 1738 he obtained the commission of an ensign in the same regiment. He thus began his career under the government that long had championed the cause of civil and religious liberty, and which was the forerunner of our own great Republic. The King of Sardinia, whose country borders on Switzerland near the home of Bouquet, became involved in a war with the combined forces of France and Spain, then leading powers of Europe. Bouquet entered the Sardinian service and distinguished himself greatly first as lieutenant, and afterwards as adjutant in several memorable and ably conducted campaigns.

At the Battle of Cony especially did he display great presence of mind and strategic talent in occupying a perilous position in such a way that his men were not aware of the imminent risk to which they were exposed. His very accurate and interesting accounts of these campaigns sent to Holland, attracted the attention of the Prince of Orange, and induced him to secure the services of Bouquet in the army of the Dutch Republic. He entered it in 1748 as captain commandant with the rank of lieutenant colonel of the Swiss guards, a regiment lately formed at The Hague.

He was sent at once with Generals Burmannia and Cornabe to receive from the French the posts in the Low Countries about to be evacuated, and the prisoners of war given up to the Republic by France at the close of the war, according to the terms of the treaty of Aix-la-Chapelle. A few months later he accepted an invitation to accompany Lord Middleton in a tour through France and Italy. It is supposed that in his intimate associations with this nobleman, Bouquet gained his surprising knowledge of the English language which he wrote better than the great majority of English officers.

# How Bouquet Spent Leisure Time

On his return to The Hague, Bouquet devoted every moment not needed in the discharge of regimental duties, to the careful study of matters pertaining to military art and tactics, especially of the higher mathematics which forms their basis. At The Hague he always moved in the best society and cultivated the friendship of the learned Professors Hemsterhius, Keening and Allamand and other leading men in every department of science.

Instead of gambling and carousing as many military men are wont to do when off active duty, Bouquet always improved his leisure moments, by enlarging his acquisitions of knowledge. At Philadelphia he was a great favourite in the most intelligent circles and enjoyed the confidential friendship of Chief Justice Allen, Benj. Chew, the Attorney General, Dr. Wm. Smith Provost of the University and Bertram the Botanist. His tastes, like his talents, were of a high order.

# Enters British Service
# Royal Americans

In 1754 war broke out between France and England on a scale that involved two continents. It was resolved to raise a corps under the name of Royal Americans consisting of four battalions each containing one thousand men. It was proposed to fill the ranks of this regiment by enlisting Protestant German and Swiss settlers in Pennsylvania and Maryland, who for the most part were unable to speak or understand the English language,

About $400,000 was voted for this purpose by Parliament. Smollet, in speaking of these German and Swiss settlers says:

> As they were all zealous Protestants and in general strong, hardy men accustomed to the climate, it was judged that a regiment of good and faithful soldiers might be raised out of them, particularly proper to oppose the French; but to this end it was necessary to appoint some officers, especially subalterns, who understood military discipline and could speak the German language; and as a sufficient number of such could not be found among the English officers it was necessary to bring over and grant commissions to several German and Swiss officers and engineers. But as this step by the Act of Settlement could not be taken without the authority of Parliament, an act was now passed for enabling his majesty to grant commissions to a certain number of foreign Protestants who had served abroad as officers or engineers to act and rank as officers

or engineers in America only.

Henry Bouquet and his intimate friend and countryman Frederick Haldiman were appointed lieutenant-colonels of this Royal American Brigade, and as colonels-*commandant* each of a thousand men were placed on an equality with the colonel-in-chief. They were allowed to select subordinate officers especially for the artillery and engineer departments, and these were chosen with rare judgement, for the most part from the lately disbanded armies of the Dutch Republic. Hence it was that such gallant soldiers and good scholars as Ecuyer, a countryman of Bouquet, obtained command in this famous regiment.

Sir Joseph Yorke major general and English minister to the Dutch Republic was mainly instrumental in the creation of this body of troops and also in securing the services of such able continental commanders as Haldimand and Bouquet. Fifty of the officers might be foreign Protestants according to the Act of Parliament, while the enlisted men were to be raised principally among the German settlers in America.

Bouquet sailed for America in the summer of 1756, the year after Braddock's disastrous defeat. Lord Loudoun was colonel of the Royal American corps and commander-in-chief of the British Army in America. Like some other British officers of Colonial days, he was haughty and blustering in peaceful communities, but very slow in facing the foe where actual danger and military duty called. As remarked by a friend of Franklin, Loudoun was like the figure of St. George, painted on the sign boards always on horseback but never riding on.

# Bouquet goes to Philadelphia

Under the orders of Loudoun Bouquet first appears in Philadelphia late in the Fall of 1756, in command of 550 officers and men, consisting of a battalion of Royal Americans and two independent companies. A demand for comfortable quarters for the troops did not meet the response from the Assembly which the Governor and British officers deemed proper, and considerable bad blood was stirred up, which, under a less judicious officer than Bouquet might have resulted disastrously to all concerned. The breach of faith on the part of the sheriff in laying the warrant for lodgings in private houses prematurely before the Assembly, almost led to a collision between the civil and military authorities. Had Loudoun himself been present at Philadelphia it is probable that the sack and pillage of part of the city would have been the outcome of this dispute. During the remainder of the winter matters moved along smoothly, and Bouquet mingled in the best intellectual and social circles of the city. tie was particularly intimate with the Shippen family and formed a very tender attachment for a Miss Anne Willing, whose mother was a Shippen. He carried on a very interesting correspondence with this young lady, even amid the cares and turmoils of the camp, verifying in a measure the sentiment of the old Castillian song.

> 'Tis the spirit most gallant in war
> That is fondest and truest in love.

In May, 1757, Bouquet was ordered to South Carolina with a detachment of Royal Americans. In September he wrote that his men were fast dying of the fever, and he seemed anxious for a more healthy location. In a quarrel that arose between Governor Lyttleton and the Assembly of South Carolina, Bancroft tells us that Bouquet successfully acted, the part of a conciliator.

# Forbes' Expedition and Dispute with Washington

Military matters were in a very lethargic state in America during 1756 and 1757, until William Pitt took the reins with a master hand and a giant's grasp. A change soon came over the face of affairs. New Jersey, New York and New England were to assist in Northern campaigns against the French. Pennsylvania and the more Southern colonies were to aid in the conquest of the West and finish the work in which Braddock so miserably failed three years previous. England was to provide arms, ammunition and tents, and even in the end, reimburse the colonies for all other expenses. With this expectation Pennsylvania went into the campaign of 1758 with great earnestness and furnished 2,700 men for the expedition against Fort Duquesne.

General John Forbes, a brave and meritorious Scotch officer, was placed in command.

Bouquet was recalled from South Carolina with his Royal Americans and given charge of the First Division, while Colonel George Washington had command of the Second Division, Virginia having furnished 2,600 troops for the campaign. Bouquet was at Fort Bedford early in July, with a part of the forces in advance of the main army. Washington was at Fort Cumberland, thirty or forty miles south of Bedford. July 25, he wrote Bouquet, earnestly advising that the expedition should advance at once by the Braddock road from Cumberland, instead of delaying to cut a road through the wilderness of Pennsylvania to Fort Duquesne.

But Bouquet did not see it in that light. He thought that a new road was demanded by the exigencies of the situation. As a military necessity, and on account of other important considerations, he proposed to cut one by as short and direct a route as possible to the Loyalhannah Creek. Washington bitterly opposed this, and some very sharp correspondence ensued on the subject. Bouquet's motives have been impugned by some writers, and it has been asserted by Hildreth that the choice was made in the interest of Pennsylvania land speculators. But he adduces no evidence to prove his assertion. It is enough to know that Bouquet's route was nearly fifty miles shorter from Bedford to Duquesne than the Cumberland route. This would commend it in a military pointy of view, and the subsequent course of events fully vindicated the wisdom of Bouquet in selecting it in spite of the strenuous opposition of the Father of our Country.

Great and good as Washington was, or afterwards became, he was still human, and, as an ardent Virginian, looked with a jealous eye upon any project that would tend to rob Virginia of her wonted prestige. His two older brothers were members of the Ohio Land Company, whose interests were at stake in this affair. Besides the monopoly of the Indian fur traffic would pass from the hands of Virginia traders, if a more direct and rival route were opened up through the province of Pennsylvania to the headwaters of the Ohio. Selfish considerations are just as likely to have influenced the one side as the other. When we recollect the long contest for the Monongahela region and a large part of Westmoreland county as originally constituted, reaching through the dark days of the Revolution, even after the new road was made, we need not wonder at the jealousy and opposition of Virginians to any project or enterprise that would in the least jeopardize their supremacy in that coveted locality.

Washington could not yield the point with a very good grace. He predicted defeat and disaster to the expedition. September 1, he writes:

> All is dwindled into ease, sloth and fatal inactivity. Nothing but a miracle can bring the campaign to a happy issue.

Bouquet convinced Forbes that, the proposed new route was preferable, and Colonel James Burd was sent forward to cut a way through the forest and erect a stockade at Loyalhannah. Colonel Armstrong, who was a captain in this expedition, wrote under date of Raystown, (Bedford) October 3, 1758, to Richard Peters:

> The general (Forbes) came here at a critical and seasonable juncture; he is weak but his spirit is good and his head clear, firmly determined to proceed as far as force and provisions will admit, which through divine favour will be far enough.
>
> The Virginians are much chagrined at the opening of the road through this government, and Colonel Washington has been a good deal sanguine and obstinate upon the occasion; but the presence of the general (Forbes) has been of great use on this as well as other accounts.
>
> Colonel Bouquet is a very sensible and useful man; notwithstanding had not the general come up the consequences would have been dangerous. I leave this place to-day as does Colonel Bouquet and some pieces of artillery.

Bouquet gave very careful instructions to Colonel Burd not to beat a drum or fire an unnecessary shot while cutting the road through the forest. In silence but with energetic dispatch the work was pushed forward. Nor did Bouquet neglect to drill his troops and keep them well in hand for the kind of fighting needed to cope with the denizens of the woods. Joseph Shippen wrote to his father from Bedford:

> Every afternoon he exercises his men in the woods and bushes in a particular manner of his own invention which will be of great service in an engagement with the Indians.

In a letter to Chief Justice Allen, written on the day of arrival at Fort Duquesne, November 25, 1758, Bouquet attributes the success of the expedition in great part to the adoption of his route. Besides being much nearer Philadelphia, the base of supplies, the route secured the favour and cooperation of the Pennsylvania German farmers on whom he had to depend for transportation and who would have been unwilling to leave their own province to follow the longer Braddock road. This contest was the beginning of the struggle for commercial supremacy which, with varying fortunes, has gone forward ever since and which now finds its leading champions in the Pennsylvania Central and Baltimore and Ohio railroads. While we would not detract one iota from the fame and merits of Washington and feel that under the circumstances it was quite natural for him to contend for what was manifestly the interest of Virginia and the Ohio land company, we yet must say that the logic of events fully vindicated the course of Bouquet and Forbes in cutting a short and direct road to Fort Duquesne.

As Pennsylvanians, at least, we should feel thankful to the firm and sagacious man who did so much to open up the western part of our state to settlement and put matters in the best possible shape for military defence along the borders. It was hard and slow work to open a wagon track through the dense forests and over towering mountains, but with an army of over 6,000 men, including many frontiersmen and woodsmen, now was the tune to have it done if the campaign was to be a complete success. Historians agree that thus twenty years were gained in the settlement of Western Pennsylvania. Forbes was a man of courage and sterling merit, and the fact that a commander such as he endorsed the Loyalhannah route, is strong proof and presumption that Bouquet had the better cause and better argument over against his indignant colleague, even the great and good Washington.

It is very probable, however, that this dispute may have contributed to the neglect or disparagement of Bouquet by biographers and historians, whose great object was to glorify the Father of our Country and present him as a hero and a sage under all circumstances, before as well as during and after the War of Independence.

Forbes was a lion hearted old Scotchman. Weak and emaciated in body but dauntless in spirit, he had himself conveyed through the wilderness on a litter between two horses. He reached Bedford September 15 but remained there six weeks waiting for the opening of the road. November 1, he arrived at the Loyalhannah. A stockade had been erected here by the road building party under Colonel Burd by direction of Colonel Bouquet. This had been assailed by the French and Indians, who made a determined sortie from Fort Duquesne to surprise and cut off the advance guard and pioneers before the main body could come up to their relief. But the assault was repulsed and in consequence the Indians became discouraged and left for their forest homes.

A reconnoitering party of 800, mostly Highlanders under Major Grant had previously pushed forward from the Loyalhannah and had gained possession of a hill in the rear of the fort, but with strange infatuation they failed to improve their advantages and opportunities. Failing to advance and surprise the garrison and making an ostentatious display they were soon surrounded by the French and Indians who shot down their huddled ranks from behind trees and ravines like so many sheep. Grant's Hill, in the centre of Pittsburg, marks the scene of this disastrous affray.

A stand made by Colonel Lewis with Provincial troops prevented the annihilation of the impracticable Scotch officer and his Highlanders who seemed to have learned nothing from Braddock's disaster or Bouquet's discipline. De Lignery cruelly gave up five of the prisoners captured in the route to be burned at the stake by the Indians and allowed the remainder to be tomahawked in cold blood on the parade ground of the fort.

Washington was directed to open the last fifty miles of the road between the Loyalhannah and Fort Duquesne. On the 24th of November, 1758, Forbes and his army were encamped at Turtle Creek, near the scene of Braddock's defeat three years before.

Provisions, forage, &c, were so nearly exhausted that some advised a retreat, but the 'iron-headed' old Scotchman, as Forbes was called, would listen to no such talk, but announced his intention of sleeping in the fort on the next night. That same evening a great smoke was seen ascending in the direction of the fort, and at midnight the camp was startled by the jar of a great explosion. The French had evacuated the post and had set fire to the magazine. They resolved to destroy what they despaired of defending. The last of their troops had embarked in boats and were seen hurrying down the Ohio as the British army approached.

The Highlanders were infuriated by the sight of the heads of slaughtered countrymen impaled on stakes along the race course as they neared the fort. These were victims of Grant's defeat. As one has said who was present, "foaming like mad boars, engaged in battle, they rushed madly on with hope to find an enemy on whom to accomplish retribution." But the detested foe was gone and gone forever was French power and prestige at the forks of the Ohio. A square stockade was built and placed in charge of Colonel Hugh Mercer with 200 men. Next year a fort was at considerable cost erected on the rums of the old fort by General Stanwix and named Fort Pitt, in honour of the English statesman, whose energetic policy had secured British supremacy in the New World. Pittsburgh was laid out at the confluence of the Allegheny and Monongahela rivers. As early as April 1761, there were 162 houses, 221 men, 73 women and 38 children in the young town of Pittsburgh, according to the returns made to Colonel Bouquet.

The capture of Fort Duquesne and the opening of the new road, proved as great a blessing to the people of Pennsylvania as Bouquet and his friends had predicted. The army speedily returned to their homes. Forbes was borne to Philadelphia, where he died a few weeks later, and was buried with great honour in Christ church.

The following extract from a letter to his lady friend at Philadelphia, written on the day of the army's arrival at the fort, shows the high estimate in which Bouquet held his hoary-headed chief:

> Fort Duquesne, *Nov. 25*, 1758.
> Dear Nancy.—I have the satisfaction to announce to you the agreeable news of the conquest of this terrible fort. The French, seized with a panic at our approach, have destroyed themselves;—that nest of Pirates which has so long harboured the murderers and destructors of our peo-

ple. They have burned and destroyed to the ground their fortifications, houses and magazines, and left us no other cover than the heavens—a very cold one for an army without tents and equipages. We bear all this hardship with alacrity, by the consideration of the immense advantage of this important acquisition.

The glory of our success must, after God, be allowed to our general, who, from the beginning, took those wise measures which deprived the French of their chief strength, and by a treaty at Easton kept such a number of Indians idle during the whole campaign and procured a peace with those inveterate enemies more necessary and beneficial than the driving of the French from the Ohio. His prudence in all his measures in the numberless difficulties he had to surmount deserves the highest praises.

# Bouquet in Command

Bouquet was now in command and by judicious conferences with the Delaware Indians and energetic management, he soon restored peace and tranquillity to the borders, so that the pioneer settlers met with little disturbance during the remainder of the French war. Four thousand settlers, who had left their homes in terror during the past few years, in consequence of the ravages that succeeded the defeat of Braddock and the cowardly retreat of Dunbar, now returned.

Bouquet, with his Royal Americans, garrisoned the forts and posts, reaching from Philadelphia *via* Carlisle, Bedford, Fort Pitt, Lake Erie, Sandusky, &c. to Detroit. This regiment, largely composed of recruits from the German and Swiss settlers of Pennsylvania and Maryland, as we have seen, held the outposts of civilization in the midst of savage beasts and savage men for seven years. Communication was kept up largely by express riders, who, taking their lives in their hands, rode rapidly from post to post.

# Byerly at Bushy Run

Andrew Byerly was induced to establish a relay station for these express riders at Bushy Run, midway between Fort Pitt and Fort Ligonier. He received a grant of several hundred acres of land from Colonel Bouquet and the proprietary government, on which he erected buildings suitable for his purpose. Here, with his second wife and a young and growing family, he settled down in the midst of the wilderness, at the end of the Penn Manor, intending to carve out a home for his children.

He cultivated friendly relations with the surrounding Indians and was soon well established, with a valuable herd of milk cows and other comforts of civilization. Here Bouquet spent many a pleasant hour in his trips to and from Fort Pitt. Ecuyer was also on friendly terms with the family. Mrs. Byerly, whose maiden name was Beatrice Guldin, had emigrated from the Canton of Berne, in Switzerland, the home of Bouquet. They often conversed about the lakes and the Alps, and friends in the far away land of their nativity and contrasted those peaceful scenes and associations with the rough experiences of pioneer life in the new world.

Byerly was a baker by profession and seems always to have been a favourite with military men. He had erected one of the very first inns ever built in Lancaster, Pa., where he resided for a long while and buried his first wife. He had baked for Braddock's army at Fort Cumberland; and, backed by Major George Washington, had beaten a Catawba warrior in a foot race, on a wager of thirty shillings, which was intended to test the relative prowess and fleetness of the two races. Afterwards he removed to Fort Bedford, where he baked for the British garrison and where his son Jacob, a great-grand-father of the writer, was born in 1760.

The garrison being small, it was not long before he located at Bushy Run, by the special favour and protection of Colonel Bouquet, on a very desirable grant along the Forbes road. The letters, written during this interval of garrison duty, from Fort Pitt, Bedford, Lancaster, &c., to his lady friend in Philadelphia, show how irksome a life of inactivity was to this man of action and of thought, and how Bouquet felt isolated among the rude soldiers and uncouth frontiersmen with whom he came in daily contact. As one who knew him well has written, "*He was a man of science and sense.*" He delighted to associate with people of intelligence and culture. He had no tastes for the vulgar pastimes and pursuits that usually occupy the time and attention of military men, when off duty, among a rude population.

Bouquet was always a welcome guest and visitor at Byerly Station, on Bushy Run, and here he seemed to unbend himself amid congenial social surroundings. His name and memory has always been cherished in the Byerly family as a precious heirloom—as a sacred legacy handed down with the benedictions of a pious and grateful ancestress.

# Pontiac's Conspiracy

The reign of peace and prosperity, which was causing the wilderness to rejoice and blossom as the rose, came to a sudden close in the spring of 1763. The French garrisons had been driven out of Canada and all their forts and posts along the St. Lawrence, the Lakes, the Ohio, the Illinois and the Mississippi had fallen into the hands of the English as a result of the capture of Fort Duquesne and Quebec. The Indians lamented the change and their spirit of discontent was fanned into a flame by disappointed French traders who led the credulous savages to believe that the great king of France would soon drive out the English and recover his lost dominion. Their easy social habits and greater tendency to enter into matrimonial relations always made the French special favourites with the red man and his daughters.

Pontiac, the great chief of the Ottawas on the shores of Lake Michigan, became the powerful exponent and champion of the spirit of hostility against the English.

He was indeed a remarkable man. He originally belonged to the Catawba Indians. Having been captured when a child and adopted by the Ottawas, he became not only the war chief but also the Sachem, or civil ruler, of his tribe by force of superior courage and ability.

He led a band of Ottawas and bore a leading part in the defeat of Braddock in 1755, along with Charles Langlade and other Lake Indians. The conduct of the British troops on that occasion caused him to have great contempt for the red coats, and he fancied that with one bold push they might be driven east of the mountains, if not into the sea. With great craft and secrecy, he laid his plans to surprise all the English forts and posts east of the mountains and massacre their Royal American garrisons. Pontiac was a born leader and had that magnetism and force of character that fitted him for the difficult and dangerous role that he resolved to play in order to restore the supremacy of the red men on the American continent. War belts had been sent among the different tribes and a general willingness manifested to unite in one mighty effort to exterminate the English.

Kiashuta or Guyasutha, a head chief of the Senecas, marshalled a part of the Five Nations to unite with the Delawares and neighbouring tribes in destroying the garrison at Fort Pitt and the smaller posts in Western Pennsylvania. But Pontiac was the leading spirit of the general movement. April 27, 1763, he held a great council on the banks of the River Ecores, near Detroit. With fierce gestures and loud, impassioned voice he denounced the English for their injustice, rapacity and arrogance. He compared and contrasted their conduct with that of the French who had always treated them as brothers.

He exclaimed:

> The red coats have conquered the French but they have not conquered us. We are not slaves or squaws, and as long as the Great Spirit is ruler we will maintain our These lakes and these woods were given us by our fathers, and we will part with them only with our lives.

He assured the council that their great father, the King of France, would soon come to their aid to win back Canada, and wreak vengeance on his enemies.

> The Indians and their French brethren would fight once more side by side as they had always fought; they would strike the English as they had struck them many moons ago, when their great army marched down the Monongahela, and they had shot them from ambush like a flock of pigeons in the woods.

The eloquence of Pontiac, backed by the harangues of other

chiefs, carried everything before it. It was agreed that a deadly blow should be struck at all the forts in the following month. Eighteen nations, or leading Indian tribes, entered into the conspiracy of which Pontiac was the head centre. The adopted Catawba lad, far from his native haunts, had become the master spirit of his race. His bugle call rallied the dusky sons of the forest from the Mississippi to the Alleghanies in one fierce phalanx of savage hostility to the red-coated British. Different parts were assigned to different leaders. The general plan, was to surprise and capture the garrison and destroy the forts in the neighbourhood of the respective tribes and then fall like a tornado upon the defenceless settlements with fire and tomahawk.

So well kept was the secret that the storm of war came like a thunderbolt from a clear sky. Nine forts and posts were captured by stratagem or assault, and their garrisons for the most part massacred. Thus, fared Le Boeuf, Venango, Presque Isle on Lake Erie, Le Bay on Lake Michigan, St. Joseph's, Miami, Ouachtanon, Sandusky and Machinaw. These, with the larger and stronger forts of Detroit, Niagara and Fort Pitt, were all attacked at about the same time.

# Siege of Detroit

The most difficult task of all, the capture of Detroit, Pontiac took in hand himself. And, no doubt, he would have succeeded at once had not his plans been betrayed by an Indian maiden to Major Gladwyn, who was in command of that important stronghold. He was forced to the alternative of a regular siege, in which he displayed wonderful fertility of resources. Several parties sent to the relief of the besieged garrison were surprised and cut off. Vessels were boarded by the savages from their canoes; immense fire rafts were floated down the river to destroy the ships of the English. The impetuous Dalzell, a friend of Putnam, and an aid of Amherst, heading a sortie or night attack upon the forces of Pontiac, was himself ambuscaded and slain with fifty-eight of his men. A thousand warriors surrounded the fort at Detroit, but Major Gladwyn had 300 good soldiers in the fort and was protected by armed vessels at anchor on the river front. Pontiac's greatest difficulty was in securing provisions for such an immense horde of savages.

A currency of birch bark with Pontiac's stamp was employed in obtaining supplies from neutral French settlers and neighbouring tribes. To his lasting honour let it be recorded that Pontiac saw to it that every piece of birch bark that bore his sign-manual was fully redeemed after the war. Not a few white individuals and communities are put to shame by the integrity, sacrifice and fidelity of the great Ottawa chieftain. He had the vices of his race, no doubt, to some extent, but their noblest virtues of courage, patience, fortitude, honesty and magnanimity were well illustrated in his character. Had he succeeded in reducing Detroit and precipitating his vast horde of besiegers upon Fort Pitt, there is little doubt but that it would have fallen and the English been driven to the sea.

Fortunately for the provinces, the great leader of the conspiracy was foiled and detained in his efforts to capture Detroit until Bouquet had routed his Eastern Confederates on the bloody field at Bushy Run, after the best contested Indian battle ever fought in the wilds of America.

# Siege of Fort Pitt and Ligonier

And now let us turn to this, the main object of our sketch. As intimated before, the Indian uprising of 1763 was a great surprise to the military and civic authorities of the land. It is true that there were signs of outbreak, but nobody dreamed that it would assume such vast proportions and be fraught with such direful consequences. The traders, who are supposed to understand Indian character and intentions better than any other class, were mostly caught in the whirlwind of disaster and overwhelmed by the suddenness of the outbreak. It was stated in the journals of that day that over one hundred traders lost their lives, and that property lost by them among the Indians or taken at the capture of the interior posts amounted to about two and a half millions of dollars. So great a loss seems hardly possible. Fort Pitt at this time was in charge of Captain Simeon Ecuyer, a brave and skilful Swiss officer, like Bouquet himself.

On the 4th of May, 1763, he wrote Bouquet that:

> Major Gladwyn writes to me that I am surrounded by rascals. He complains a great deal of the Delawares and Shawanees. It is this *canaille* who stir up the rest to mischief.

On the 27th a party of Indians encamped near the fort and offered to trade a great quantity of valuable furs for bullets, hatchets, gunpowder, &c. They were looked upon with suspicion. On the 29th of May Ecuyer wrote an important letter to Bouquet, which seems to have been about the last that got through before communication was cut off; for on the 17th of June Lieutenant Blane, commanding at Fort Ligonier wrote Bouquet that he had heard nothing from Fort Pitt since May 30. No further tidings were received until Bouquet cut his way through in August.

The following is Captain Ecuyer's letter in full, a copy of which, in the original French, as well as an English translation, has been kindly furnished the writer by Francis Parkman, the historian of Pontiac, &c.

Fort Pitt, *May 29,* 1763.

Sir.—A large party of Mingoes arrived at the beginning of the month and gave up to us ten horses of poor quality. They asked me for presents, but I refused everything they had to offer except eight *merits* of Indian corn, (*i.e.*: 24 bushels, C. C.,) which they planted opposite Crogan's house, where they have built a town. In the evening of the day before yesterday, Mr. McKee reported to me that the Mingoes and Delawares were in motion and had sold in a great hurry skins to the value of £300., with which they bought as much powder and lead as they pleased.

Yesterday I sent him to their towns to get information, but he found them entirely abandoned, and followed their trail and is certain that they have gone down the river, which makes me think that they want to interrupt our boats and close the passage against us. They stole three horses and a cask of rum at Bushy Run. They even robbed a man named Coleman of £50, (on the Bedford road,) holding their guns against his body. I am assured that the famous Wolfe and Butler were the chiefs; it is clear that they want to break with us.

I pity the poor people on the communication. I am at work to put this post in the best position possible with the few people I have. Just as I was finishing my letter, three men came from Clapham's with the melancholy news that yesterday, at three o'clock in the afternoon, the Indians murdered Clapham and everybody in his house. These three men were at work outside and escaped through the woods. I gave them arms and sent them to aid our people at Bushy Run. The Indians have told Byerly ( at Bushy Run) to leave his house within four days, or he and all his family would be murdered. I tremble for the small posts. As for this one, I will answer for it.

S. Ecuyer.

If you do not often get letters from me, it will be a proof that the communication is cut.

To Colonel Bouquet.

From this time until the tenth of August, the garrison was cooped up in the fort, and communications cut off.

# The Flight of the Byerlys to Fort Ligonier

Let us take another look at Bushy Run before we dwell upon the siege of Fort Pitt.

As Ecuyer states, Byerly had received warning, but his family was in no condition to be moved. Mrs. Byerly had just been confined and the departure was delayed as long as possible, indeed until certain death was imminent if the flight should be any longer postponed. Byerly had gone with a small party (perhaps Clapham's men referred to above) to bury some persons who had been killed at some distance from his station. A friendly Indian who had often received a bowl of milk and bread from Mrs. Byerly came to the house after dark and informed the family that they would all be killed if they did not make their escape before daylight. Mrs. Byerly got up from her sick couch and wrote the tidings on the door of the house for the information of her husband when he should return. A horse was saddled on which the mother with her tender babe three day's old in her arms was placed, and a child not two years old was fastened behind her.

Michael Byerly was a good-sized lad, but Jacob was only three years old and had a painful stone bruise on one of his feet. With the aid of his older brother who held him by the hand and sometimes carried him on his back, the little fellow, however, managed to make good time through the wilderness to Fort Ligonier about thirty miles distant. But although he reached his ninety-ninth year he never forgot that race for life in his childhood, nor did he feel like giving quarters to hostile Indians, one of whom he killed on an island in the Alleghany in a fight under Lieutenant Hardin in 1779, although the savage begged for quarters.

Milk cows were highly prized by frontier families in those days, and the Byerly family made a desperate effort to coax and drive their small herd along to Fort Ligonier. But the howling savages got so close that they were obliged to leave the cattle in the woods to be destroyed by the Indians. Byerly in some way eluded the Indians and joined his family in the retreat. They barely escaped with their lives. The first night they spent in the stockade, and in the morning the bullets of the pursuers struck the gates as the family pressed into the fort. Here they were compelled to remain two months, exposed to great privations and repeated assaults of Indians. Fort Pitt would have been nearer and preferable as a place of safety had it been possible to reach it. As it was they had to choose the longer road and the weaker fort as the only chance of escape from the red demons. At Fort Pitt Captain Ecuyer put everything in the best possible shape for defence. The garrison consisted of 330 soldier, traders and backwoodsmen, who were armed and drilled for the emergency. There were also about one hundred women in the fort and a still greater number of children.

A hospital was constructed under the drawbridge, out of range of musket shot, for patients suffering from smallpox, and the captain was very apprehensive that disease would break out in epidemic form as a result of the overcrowded condition of the fort. He seemed to have no fear of losing the fort. A letter, written at the time, says:

> We are in such a good posture of defence that with God's assistance we can defend it against a thousand Indians.

Careful preparation was made for an attack. Buildings outside of the ramparts were levelled to the ground, and every morning at an hour before dawn the drum beat and the troops were ordered to their alarm posts. A heavy guard was kept on duty night and day. The brave and judicious Ecuyer wrote to Bouquet:

I am determined to hold my post, spare my men and never expose them without necessity. This is what I think you require of me.

It was next thing to death to expose a head on the ramparts, or to wander outside the fortification. Lurking savages were at hand to pick off the unwary. On the 25th of June, the Indians captured a lot of horses and cattle, belonging to the fort. A general fire was then opened on the fort from all sides. A discharge of howitzers threw them into confusion and made them act more cautiously. Next morning, Turtle Heart, a Delaware chief, approached the fort in the guise of friendship, and advised the commander and garrison to withdraw and take the women and children down to the English settlements, in order to escape destruction from the six great nations of Indians, who were coming to destroy them. He promised that they would be protected in making their escape. This was the ruse by which so many traders and smaller posts had been deceived and finally treacherously murdered after they had given up their arms. But Ecuyer was not to be caught with such chaff. He replied in a very ironical way, thanking the Delaware brothers for their great kindness, and assuring them that he and his troops could hold the fort against all the Indians that dared to attack it. He said:

We are very well off in this place, and we mean to stay.

He then told them in confidence that two great armies were coming, one from the East and the other from the Lakes, to destroy the bad Indians, while the Cherokees and Catawbas, their old enemies were joining a third army in Virginia to destroy them. This speech seemed to have a demoralizing effect upon the savages, who withdrew for a season to meet a large body of warriors approaching from the west. During this interval Ensign Price, from Fort Le Boeuf, entered Fort Pitt with his command of a dozen men, who had gallantly defended their little post until it was in flames from burning arrows and had then cut their way out of the rear and escaped after great peril and suffering.

The names of this detachment of Royal Americans, as far as given, indicate their German descent, *viz*.: Fisher, Nash, Do-good, Nigley, Dortinger and Trunk. Captain Ecuyer strengthened his defences with a line of palisades and constructed a rude fire engine to extinguish flames caused by the burning arrows of the Indians shot against the sides and roofs of wooden buildings. July 26, a small party of Indians came to parley, under the lead of Shingas and Turtle Heart. They professed great affection for the whites, and great concern for their safety. The Ottawas were coming in great force from Detroit to destroy the garrison, and they begged their white brothers to depart while it could be done in safety.

Ecuyer replied that he could defend the fort for three years against all the Indians in the woods, and that he would never abandon it as long as a white man lived in America. He despised the Ottawas and warned his Delaware brothers to keep out of reach of his bombshells and cannon loaded with a whole bag full of bullets. Thwarted in their crafty and treacherous schemes by which they had succeeded in destroying Lieutenant Gordon and his entire command at Venango, the Indians began a general attack in earnest. Many of them dug holes in the river banks, from which to fire on the fort, and from all sides bullets and arrows flew thick and fast. The Royal Americans and border riflemen from their loopholes drew a bead on every Indian that exposed his person in the least.

Ecuyer was wounded in the leg by an arrow but kept up the hopes and spirits of his men, while at the same time he refused to let them sally forth to engage in a hand to hand conflict with the savages, as many of them proposed to do. The attack lasted five days and five nights.

Ecuyer speaks with great admiration of the conduct of his men—regulars and the rest:

> I am fortunate to have the honour of commanding such brave men. I only wish the Indians had ventured an assault. They would have remembered it to the thousandth generation.

Bouquet wrote General Amherst, August 11, in terms of high praise of Ecuyer for the defence of the fort and the important additions made to the fortifications during the investment.

In various letters, written from the fort immediately after the siege was raised, it is stated that:

> To a man they were resolved to defend the position (if the troops had not arrived ) as long as any ammunition and provisions to support them was left; and that then they would have fought their way through or died in the attempt, rather than have been made prisoners by such perfidious, cruel and bloodthirsty hell-hounds. Some of the women in the fort, it is said, helped to defend the place. Many express-riders going to and from the garrison have been killed.

# Defence of Fort Ligonier

At Fort Ligonier matters were even more critical than at Fort Pitt. The stockade was bad and the garrison extremely weak but Byerly and a few other frontier settlers had made their way into it with their families and helped to repulse the assaults of the savages. Lieutenant Archibald Blane with a detachment of Royal Americans was in command and conducted the defence with great courage and practical tact.

On the 4th of June Blane writes:

> Thursday last my garrison was attacked by a body of Indians, about five in the morning; but as they only fired upon us from the skirts of the woods, I contented myself with giving them three cheers, without spending a single shot upon them. But as they still continued their popping upon the side next to the town, I sent the sergeant of the Royal Americans with a proper detachment to fire the houses, which effectually disappointed them in their plan.

On the 17th, he writes to Bouquet,

> I hope soon to see yourself and live in daily hopes of a reinforcement. Sunday last a man straggling out was killed by the Indians.
> I believe the communication between Fort Pitt and this place is entirely cut off, not having heard from them since the thirtieth of May, though two expresses have gone from Bedford to that post.

On the 21st the Indians made a serious attack for two hours.

A small party of fifteen men were so exceedingly anxious to have a closer tilt with the savages that the lieutenant finally yielded to their entreaties to let them out to attack some Indians that showed themselves at a little distance. As it turned out this was only a decoy to entrap them. About a hundred savages lay in ambush by the side of the creek about four hundred yards from the fort; and just as the party was returning near where they lay, the savages rushed out to cut them off and would have succeeded in doing so had it not been for a deep morass which intervened. Foiled in this movement, more by natural obstacles then by the judgement or sagacity of the whites, the Indians immediately began an attack upon the fort and fired upwards of a thousand shots without doing any special damage.

Bouquet was deeply concerned for the safety of Fort Ligonier, for on its preservation depended the safety of Fort Pitt and his own army of deliverance. A large quantity of military stores were in the magazines at Ligonier, with which the Indians might have blown up Fort Pitt or reduced Bouquet's troops to the greatest extremities. A picked party of thirty Highlanders was sent by a circuitous route through the woods travelling by night at their utmost speed under the escort of experienced guides. They got close to the fort without being discovered and then by a sudden rush and a running fight they managed to get in without losing a man. This was a timely relief and ensured the safety of the post until the main body could arrive.

Next to Ligonier in the line of communication came Fort Bedford, at a distance of fifty miles across the mountains and through the wilderness. Captain Lewis Ourry was in command here with a mere handful of Royal Americans. On the third of June he wrote Bouquet that owing to the arrival of express riders, (who were generally soldiers sent from one post to another at the peril of their lives,) his regulars were increased to "three corporals and nine privates." But he had a large body of settlers who, frightened by depredations of the Indians in the neighbourhood, rushed pell-mell to the fort. These he organised into two military companies, aggregating 150 men. Over one hundred families had sought refuge at the fort.

When the scare was over for the time being the silly people would venture out in small squads, and many were thus cut off and slain by scalping parties of skulking savages. June seventh, he writes,

> I long to see my Indian scouts come in with intelligence; but I long more to hear the Grenadiers march and see more red-coats.

Ten days later the country people in fancied security had returned to their plantation so that Ourry was left alone with a garrison of only twelve Royal Americans, who had not only to guard the fort but likewise take care of seven Indian prisoners. He writes to Bouquet:

> I should be very glad to see some troops come to my assistance. A fort with five bastions cannot be guarded much less defended by a dozen men, but I hope God will protect us.

The killing and scalping of some families on Denning's creek threw the settlers into a panic again, and in a few days the militia were back from their farms and with difficulty could be prevented from murdering the Indian prisoners. Ourry feared that the Indians, despairing of taking Fort Pitt, would fall upon and destroy the smaller posts and ravage the settlements, which they doubtless would have done had Bouquet's advance been much longer delayed.

July 2nd, about twenty Indians attacked a party of mowers and killed several of them. Eighteen persons in all were killed near Fort Bedford. July 3, Ourry received word from Blane of the loss of Presque Isle on Lake Erie, Le-Boeuf, Venango, &c, which he sends to Bouquet with the intimation that Blane had entertained some idea of evacuating or capitulating Fort Ligonier. Bouquet replied:

> I shivered when you hinted to me Lieutenant Bl—'s intentions. Death and infamy would have been the reward he would expect instead of the honour he has obtained by his prudence, courage and resolution. This is a most trying

time. You may be sure that all the expedition possible will be used for the relief of the few remaining posts.

Parkman remarks on the above letter:

> Bouquet had the strongest reason for wishing that Fort Ligonier should hold out. As the event showed its capture would probably have entailed the defeat and destruction of his entire command.

# The Situation at Carlisle

Bouquet had his headquarters in Philadelphia as Colonel of the first battalion of Royal Americans at the time of the outbreak of Pontiac and his confederates. His Royal Americans, broken into detachments, had held the line of forts and posts between that place and Detroit for over six years. As military hermits they held the outposts of civilization in the Western wilderness. Bouquet, as we have seen, was held in high esteem in Philadelphia.

He was in the prime of life, had a fine personal presence, splendid physique and extraordinary qualities of mind and heart.

> Firmness, integrity, calmness, presence of mind in the greatest of dangers—virtues so essential to a commander, were natural to him. His presence inspired confidence and impressed respect, encouraged his friends and confounded his foes.

Such is the estimate given of Bouquet by some of the best men of the provinces who knew him well. He promptly reported the situation to General Amherst as Ecuyer had informed him in letters written at the end of May. The haughty and arrogant Briton could not believe that the despicable savages would be so audacious as to besiege his forts or attack regular troops of equal numbers with their own. It is amusing to read his brag and bluster and to mark the change which in some respects seems to come over the spirit of his dream as the campaign progresses.

Bouquet evidently knew his weak and strong points and knew how to secure his hearty co-operation in measures necessary to the success of the beleaguered garrisons.

June 23, Amherst ordered Major Campbell to proceed at once from New York to Philadelphia with the remains of the 42nd Regiment of Royal Highlanders, and of the 77th Montgomery's Highlanders; the first consisting of two hundred and fourteen men, including officers, and the latter of one hundred and thirty-three. These troops had just landed from the West Indies and were in a very emaciated condition, most of them really unfit for service. The remains of five more such regiments arrived from Havana July 29, numbering in all nine hundred and eighty-two men and officers fit for duty; but by this time Bouquet was beyond Fort Bedford. Amherst seemed incapable of comprehending the magnitude of the danger. He writes to Bouquet:

> If you think it necessary you will yourself proceed to Fort Pitt that you may be better enabled to put in execution the requisite orders for securing the communication and reducing the Indians to reason.

Bouquet was not the man to shirk duty or danger in such a crisis. With all the energy of his ardent and indomitable nature he threw himself into the work of preparing an expedition for the relief of the invested forts and the exposed frontiers. He sent forward orders for the collection of stores and transportation at Carlisle as soon as the outlook became serious.

After making the necessary arrangements at Philadelphia, he hastened toward Carlisle. At Lancaster he writes to Amherst expressing confidence in his ability to open up communication with the troops sent to his assistance.

Amherst replies:

> I wish to hear of no prisoners, should any of the villains be met with in arms.

On the 3rd of July Bouquet received what he calls:

> The fatal account of the loss of our posts at Presque Isle, Le-Boeuf and Venango.

The express rider who brought the message from Bedford

came through in one day. He told the disastrous news to the country people who flocked about him and remarked, as he rode towards Bouquet's tent, "the Indians will be here soon."

All was consternation and alarm. Word was sent out to the settlements and soon every road was filled with panic-stricken fugitives crowding into Carlisle. The Indians were raiding through the Juniata regions and along the borders of the Cumberland valley. A scouting party found Shearman's valley laid waste, the dwellings and stacked grain on fire, and swine devouring the bodies of slaughtered settlers. Twelve young men went to warn the people of the Tuscarora valley. They found the work of ruin in full blast already and fell into an ambush in which they were nearly all killed.

The country between the mountains and the Susquehanna was abandoned. Two thousand families left their homes and fled to the forts and larger towns for protection.

A letter written from Carlisle, July 5, 1763, gives us an idea of the terrible panic which existed:

> Nothing could exceed the terror which prevailed from house to house and from town to town. The road was near covered with women and children flying to Lancaster and Philadelphia.
> The Rev. ———, pastor of the Episcopal church, went at the head of his congregation to protect and encourage them on the way. A few retired to the breastworks for safety. The alarm once given could not be appeased.
> We have done all that men can do to prevent disorder. All our hopes are turned upon Bouquet.

Instead of finding supplies at hand for his troops and for the relief of the forts, Bouquet found a vast crowd of despairing and starving people, while crops were being burnt and mills destroyed on all sides. July 13th, Bouquet wrote Amherst from Carlisle as follows:

> The list of the people, known to be killed, increases very fast every hour. The desolation of so many families reduced to the last extremity of want and misery; the despair

of those who have lost their parents, relations and friends, with cries of distracted women and children who fill the streets—form a scene painful to humanity and impossible to describe.

To procure provisions, horses and wagons under the circumstances was indeed a herculean task.

A few friendly Indians at the fort he with difficulty saved from the fury of the mob of rustics. Instead of helping him forward the settlers were rather a drawback and encumbrance and had to be fed from the public crib.

# The March to Bedford

However, in 18 days after his arrival at Carlisle, by judicious and energetic measures, a convoy was procured and the army set out on its perilous march.

His entire force did not exceed 500 men, of whom the most effective were the 42nd Highlanders. Sixty of the 77th Regiment were so weak that they had to be conveyed in wagons. They were intended for garrison duty at Bedford &c., while effective men at those forts were to join the army of deliverance. The bare-legged Highlanders with their kilts and plaids, and their infirm appearance, gave little assurance to the anxious people who watched their departure.

The fate of Braddock a few years previous had not been forgotten, nor the desolation and despair that ensued. Nearly twice as many English troops had been slain on that fatal day as Bouquet had in his entire command, while the Indians that now infested the woods were far more numerous than those who routed the proudest of the Britons eight years previous.

At Shippensburg, as at Carlisle, a great crowd of starving people were found, who had fled from the tomahawk and scalping knife. On July 25, 1763 there were in Shippensburg 1384 of our poor distressed back inhabitants, *viz*: 301 men, 345 women and 738 children, many of whom were obliged to lie in barns, stables, cellars and under old leaky sheds, the dwelling houses being all crowded, says the chronicles of those days. In such a state of affairs it would seem that the provincial authorities and frontiersmen themselves would have united in one grand effort to drive out the savage destroyers of life and property. But Bouquet could get little or no aid from that quarter.

A suicidal Quaker policy pervaded the civil authorities, while the settlers seemed benumbed with fear and despondency.

He writes to Amherst:

> I find myself utterly abandoned by the very people I am ordered to protect I have borne very patiently the ill usage of this province, having still hopes that they will do something for us; and therefore, have avoided a quarrel with them.

His efforts to engage a body of frontiersmen for the campaign were fruitless. They preferred to remain for the defence of their families, forgetting that their homes and families could never be secure until the savages had been driven back to their haunts beyond the Ohio and chastised into submission. Such a force of men, used to the woods and enured to pioneer life, would have been of vast service in the march.

The Highlanders were sure to get lost in the woods when sent out as flankers. As Bouquet wrote to Amherst July 26:

> I cannot send a Highlander out of my sight without running the risk of losing the man, which exposes me to surprises from the skulking villains I have to deal with.

Doubtless, however, the tactics resorted to in 1758 to make his men effective against Indian attack and surprise during the Forbes campaign, were called into vigorous play during this march, as the outcome at Bushy Run clearly indicates. At Bedford, where he arrived July 25, Bouquet was more fortunate in enlisting frontiersmen and succeeded in getting about thirty to march with the army for flanking and scouting purposes.

Murders had continued in the settlements; three men having been killed near Shippensburg by prowling savages after the army passed. But thus far the troops had met with little molestation.

# The March to Ligonier

Now, however, began the real perils of the march, and greater caution was needed. Forests, rocks, ravines and thickets abounded on every side, inviting their wily foe to ambush the troops as they threaded their way through the valleys and across the mountains.

But Bouquet knew exactly what the exigencies of the situation required. July 28, the army started from Fort Bedford. A band of backwoodsmen led the way, followed closely by the pioneers; the wagons and cattle were in the centre guarded by the regulars and a. rear guard of backwoodsmen closed up the line. Frontier riflemen, or provincial rangers, scoured the woods on all sides, making prise impossible. Bouquet himself, with musket in hand oftentimes led the advance. Thus, they toiled along the tedious way, which Burd, under Bouquet's orders, had opened through the wilderness five years before.

The mountain air the pure water and delightful scenery had an inspiring effect upon the Highlanders, who grew stronger as they marched along.

August 2, the little garrison and small body of pioneer settlers, who had held Fort Ligonier for two long months, were transported with the sight of the red coats of the Royal Americans and the kilts and plaids of the Highlanders marching to their rescue.

"The Campbells were coming" indeed, as the record of the bloody fight a few days later fully demonstrates. The clan Campbell, whose members have marched so oft in many lands to glory and the grave, was well represented in the rank and file of

# Bouquet's Army of Deliverance

The Indians disappeared as the troops approached, but no tidings had been received from Fort Pitt for weeks. Bouquet wisely resolved to leave his wagons and oxen behind, which were the most cumbrous part of his convoy, in order to advance more rapidly and be in better shape to resist attack. Three hundred and forty pack horses were loaded with supplies for the needy garrison at Fort Pitt, and on the 4th day of August the army marched about a dozen miles and encamped for the night.

Andrew Byerly and his son Michael accompanied the troops, in hopes of recovering some of their property, which had been left to the mercy of the Indians when the family had fled from Bushy Run over two months ago. After proceeding a few miles, the boy was sent back for some reason, to remain at Fort Ligonier. On his return he saw numerous Indian trails crossing the dusty road, over which the army had passed. The savages were on were on the alert to ascertain the number and character of the troops and watching their opportunity to surprise and ambush them.

Bouquet had his plans well arranged for the speedy relief of Fort Pitt in a way that would be most likely to thwart the designs of the savages. His intention was to push on to Bushy Run, which would be an excellent place for man and beast to rest and recuperate for a few hours, and then set out and make a forced march by night through the denies at Turtle Creek, where he expected the savages would try to ambuscade his troops.

# Bushy Run Battle

Accordingly, on the morning of August 5, 1763, the troops set out at an early hour over the hills, and through the hollows of what now forms the heart of Westmoreland County, Pa. Along the Forbes road, shrouded on all sides by dense forests, they moved at a lively rate. By one o'clock the jaded column had advanced seventeen miles, and Andrew Byerly, along with a detachment of eighteen soldiers in the advance, cheered the weary troops with the welcome tidings that Bushy Run, their resting place, was only half a mile distant. All were pushing forward with renewed vigour, when suddenly the whole line was startled by the report of rifles in the front. A fierce assault had been made on the vanguard and the firing was quick and sharp. Twelve out of eighteen fell in the unequal conflict that ensued before the two advance companies could press forward to the relief of their comrades. The firing became furious, indicating that the Indians were in large force and were fighting with unusual courage.

The convoy of packhorses was halted, the troops were formed into line and a general bayonet charge was made through the forest. The yelping savages gave way before the cold steel of the Highlanders. But just as the route seemed cleared in front, terrible war whoops resounded through the woods on either flank, and an uproar among the packhorse drivers indicated that the convoy was attacked in the rear. The troops in advance were instantly recalled to defend the convoy. Driving away the savages by repeated bayonet charges they formed a circle around the crowded and frantic horses. It was a new kind of work for the Highlanders, but they bore themselves with great steadiness and remarkable fortitude in spite of the terrific and confusing yells of their ferocious assailants and the deadly shots that came pouring in upon them from every thicket, tree or covert, large enough to conceal a foe. Nothing but implicit confidence in their commander and in the pluck and fidelity of each other could account for their undaunted gallantry under such trying circumstances. It seemed like pandemonium broke loose. Walter Scott has described such a scene:

*At once there rose so wild a yell*
*Within that dark and narrow dell,*
*As all the fiends from heaven that fell,*
*Had pealed the banner-cry of hell.*

Rushing up with terrific whoops, the painted demons would pour in a heavy fire, and when the Highlanders would charge bayonet they would dodge and vanish behind trees and thickets only to renew the assault the moment the troops returned toward the circle of defence.

Many brave men fell on that hot afternoon. Captain Lieutenant Graham and Lieutenant McIntosh of the 42nd Highlanders were killed and Lieutenant Graham wounded. Lieutenant Donald Campbell of the 77th was wounded and Lieutenant Dow, of the Royal Americans, was shot through the body, after killing three Indians.

Upwards of sixty men were killed or wounded in the action which lasted until dark. It was impossible to change and the troops were obliged to lay upon their arms where they had stood during the fight. Numerous sentinels were posted to guard against a night attack. A space was made in the centre of the camp for the wounded, around whom a wall of flour bags was erected to protect them from the bullets which flew among them thick and fast from all side during the fight. It was indeed a sad and dreary night for the wounded.

The agony of thirst was almost intolerable, springs ran out of the hill sides nearby, but the savages guarded them well with their skirmish line, and it was almost certain death to approach them. At imminent risk Byerly managed to convey a few hatfulls of water to the wounded Highlanders. A grateful shower of rain also afforded some relief. After Bouquet had made his dispositions for the night he proceeded to write a report of the battle to General Amherst, evidently supposing that he was not likely to survive the conflict the coming day. The report was written amid all the bustle of the camp when danger and death in their most horrid forms stared him in the face, and yet how carefully, calmly and correctly everything of note is stated! Here it is.

# Report of the First Day's Fight Near Bushy Run

Camp at Edge Hill,
26 Miles from Fort Pitt, 5th Aug. 1763.

Sir: The second instant the troops and convoy arrived at Ligonier, where I could obtain no intelligence of the enemy. The expresses sent since the beginning of July, having been either killed or obliged to return, all the passes being occupied by the enemy. In this uncertainty, I determined to leave all the wagons, with the powder, and a quantity of stores and provisions, at Ligonier, and on the 4th proceeded with the troops and about 340 horses loaded with flour.

I intended to have halted today at Bushy Run, (a mile beyond this camp), and after having refreshed the men and horses, to have marched in the night over Turtle Creek, a very dangerous defile of several miles, commanded by high and rugged hills; but at one o'clock this afternoon, after a march of seventeen miles, the savages suddenly attacked our advance guard, which was immediately supported by the two Light Infantry companies of the 42nd Regiment, who drove the enemy from their ambuscade and pursued them a good way.

The savages returned to the attack, and the fire being obstinate on our front and extending along our flanks, we made a general charge with the whole line to dislodge the savages from the heights, in which attempt we succeeded, without by it obtaining any decisive advantage, for as soon as they were driven from one post, they appeared on another, till by continued reinforcements, they were at last able to surround us and attacked the convoy left in our rear; this obliged us to march back to protect it.

The action then became general, and though we were attacked on every side, and the savages exerted themselves with uncommon resolution, they were constantly repulsed with loss; we also suffered considerably. Captain Lieutenant Graham and Lieutenant James McIntosh, of the 42nd, are killed, and Captain Graham wounded. Of the Royal American Regt., Lieutenant Dow. who acted as A. D. O. M. G., is shot through the body.

Of the 77th, Lieutenant Donald Campbell and Mr. Peebles, a volunteer, are wounded. Our loss in men, including rangers and drivers, exceeds sixty killed or wounded.

The action has lasted from one o'clock till night, and we expect to begin at daybreak.

Whatever our fate may be, I thought it necessary to give your Excellency this early information, that you may at all events take such measures as you think proper with the Provinces, for their own safety, and the effectual relief of Fort Pitt, as in case of another engagement, I fear insurmountable difficulties in protecting and transporting our provisions, being already so much weakened by the losses of this day in men and horses, besides the additional necessity of carrying the wounded, whose situation is truly deplorable.

I cannot sufficiently acknowledge the constant assistance I have received from Major Campbell during this long action, nor express my admiration of the cool and steady behaviour of the troops, who did not fire a shot without orders, and drove the enemy from their posts with fixed bayonets. The conduct of the officers is much above my praises.

I have the honour to be with great respect,
Sir, &c. Henry Bouquet,

RETURN OF KILLED AND WOUNDED IN THE TWO ACTIONS AT EDGE HILL, NEAR BUSHY RUN, THE FIFTH AND SIXTH AUGUST, 1763.

| CORPS. | Captains. | | Lieuts. | | Volunt'rs. | | Serge'nts, Corporals, Drum'rs. | | Privates. | | |
|---|---|---|---|---|---|---|---|---|---|---|---|
| | Killed | Wounded | Killed | Wounded | Killed | Wounded | Killed | Wounded | Killed | Wounded | Missing |
| 42d Regt. Royal Highlanders, | 1 | 1 | 2 | 3 | .. | .. | 1 | 4 | 25 | 25 | .. |
| 60th Regt. Royal Americans, | .. | .. | .. | 1 | .. | 1 | .. | .. | 6 | 4 | .. |
| 77th Regt. Montgomery's Highlanders, | .. | .. | .. | 1 | .. | .. | 2 | 3 | 5 | 7 | .. |
| Volunteers, Rangers and Pack horse men, | .. | .. | 1 | .. | .. | .. | .. | .. | 7 | 8 | 5 |
| Total, | 1 | 1 | 2 | 3 | .. | 1 | 2 | 5 | 43 | 40 | 5 |

KILLED—Captain Lieut. John Graham, of the 42d Regiment; Lieut. James McIntosh, of the 42d Regiment; Lieut. Joseph Randall, of the Rangers.
WOUNDED—Captain John Graham, of the 42d Regiment; Lieut. Duncan Campbell, of the 42d Regiment; Lieut. Donald Campbell, of the 77th Regiment; Volunteer, Mr. Peebles, of the 77th Regiment.

Total Killed, .................................................... 50
" Wounded, .................................................... 60
" Missing, ...................................................... 5

Total of the whole, .................................................... 115

To His Excellency, Sir Jeffrey Amherst.

With gloomy forebodings the troops, and especially the wounded, awaited the dawn of the coming day. Wild whoops and occasional shots from the deep thickets and surrounding hillsides, indicated how eager the painted demons were to glut their vengeance. The hordes besieging Fort Pitt had all precipitated themselves upon Bouquet, knowing that if he and his supplies could be cut off and captured, the reduction of the fort would soon follow. It was a very disturbed and broken sleep that even the most securely sheltered of the troops could get at such a time.

# Second Day's Fight, August 6

With the first gray streaks of dawn came those incessant savage yells preluding a fierce assault on every side. Soon from every tree and bush that could conceal an enemy, a galling fire was poured upon the devoted forces of Bouquet. The colonel himself, with his bright uniform, was a conspicuous mark, and the balls whizzed about him so thick that he concluded to change his dress. While doing so, behind a large tree, no less than fourteen bullets struck it. As on the previous day, the savages made frequent impetuous onsets in order to break through the line of defence. But they were firmly met and gallantly repulsed at every point. The gleam of the bayonets would cause them to retire swiftly to the bushes, but the moment the charge ceased they were back again with their demoniac yells, popping away at every exposed soldier. The long march and hard fight of the previous day, added to their burning thirst, "more intolerable than the enemy's fire," as Bouquet puts it, left the troops in rather sorry plight to contend with such alert and daring assailants.

The Indians had every advantage on their side in the way of shelter from the fire of the troops and being without any encumbrance they could attack and retreat with the greatest ease and rapidity. The savages marked the increasing fatigue and distress of the troops and, confident of speedy triumph, derided them in bad English and vulgar ribaldry. Kukyuskung, a Delaware chief, who had taken part in the murder of Colonel Clapham and his family, and who was a ringleader in getting up the conspiracy in general, was conspicuous in this kind of work throughout the morning, as he had been also on the previous night. His taunts were all the more provoking, as he bellowed them forth from behind a large tree, because he had, in times past, received many favours from Colonel Bouquet and the Royal Americans, when on his visits to Fort Pitt.

The interior of the camp was in great confusion owing to the fright of horses on account of the terrific war whoops resounding on all sides and the hurts received from Indian bullets. The cowardly behaviour of the pack horse men added to the danger and tumult. They forsook the poor brutes and hid themselves in terror among the bushes, from which no command or entreaty could draw them to a discharge of duty. Breaking away from the convoy many of the horses dashed madly through the woods, and through the lines of the contending forces.

The crisis was fearful and only a cool head, fertile in resources and a brave heart unappalled by any danger, could meet the emergency. The heat, the toil, the thirst, the increasing and more audacious assaults of the savages began to tell seriously upon the strength and spirits of the soldiers They were growing weaker and falling rapidly while their relentless foes were every moment growing stronger and bolder.

It was a crisis requiring the highest kind of military genius combined with indomitable resolution. Bouquet was equal to the ordeal and from the very jaws of defeat, disaster and death he snatched the most brilliant victory ever won over the Indians.

A Captain or, Lieutenant Barret, commanding it is said a small Maryland detachment of provincial rangers, pointed out to Bouquet a place where a large body of the boldest of the Indians might be taken on the flank and rear by a well-directed bayonet charge around the hill and up a hollow or ravine. Andrew Byerly was with Bouquet at the time and heard Barret make the suggestion, which the colonel quickly put into execution on a large scale by a masterly piece of strategy.

Immediately Major Campbell was directed to make a rapid circuit through the woods on the right flank of the savages around the hill aforesaid, taking them in flank and rear. Captain Basset of the Royal Engineers was directed to arrange the other companies, so as to co-operate promptly with the strategic movement at the right moment. The thin line of troops that took the place of the two companies withdrawn from the front, gave away before the impetuous onset of the exultant savages and fell back upon the convoy, where they presented a line of bristling steel. The Indians fell completely into the snare and rushed with demoniac fury into the camp, certain that the fight was won.

But just as they supposed themselves masters of the field the Highlanders charged in with a wild battle cry upon their right flank. A volley was fired upon the amazed and huddled savages, but they stood their ground with wonderful intrepidity, not willing to lose a decisive victory and the great booty of stores and scalps which a moment before they felt was within their grasp. It is agreed on all hands that on this occasion, not only in the attack and the assault, but in meeting the unexpected charge on their flank and rear, the Indians displayed unusual courage and firmness.

But a well-directed bayonet charge, no body of Indians ever did or will stand. Here Bouquet had them at last where he wanted them, at close quarters where there could be no dodging or popping from behind the trees. The Highlanders were at home with the bayonet and only too glad to get a good chance at the painted villains who had skulked behind trees while they shot their brave comrades during the past two days. but the savages struggled in hope of gaining the day, but the shock was irresistible and, perceiving that they had been caught in a trap, they fled in tumultuous disorder. In doing so they were obliged to pass in front of the companies brought up on the opposite side by Captain Basset, from whom they received another volley. The four companies now vied with each other in driving the savages through the woods beyond Bushy Run without giving them time to reload their empty rifles. Many of their chief warriors were killed and the rest utterly routed. Among others, Kukyuskung, the ungrateful and blatant blackguard, and the famous war chief called "The Wolf," were slain.

Amherst had expressed the hope that no prisoners with arms in their hands should be taken, and his wish was gratified. Historians say that in the fight only one Indian was taken prisoner, and after a little examination he was shot down like a captured wolf.

Hereby hangs a tale, which I was told by my great great grandfather, Jacob Byerly, and his son Joseph, on Christmas day 1855, two and a half years before the old Revolutionary veteran passed away, at the age of 99 years. He had heard it often from his father, who was in the fight. When the night of the savages had fairly begun, a Scotch Highlander dropped his musket and darted after the fugitives, as only a fleet-footed Highlander could. Soon he overtook and mastered, single-handed, one of the largest of the savages, whom he was leading toward the camp, when he was met by an officer of Barret's detachment.

"What are you going to do with that fellow?" said the fussy official.

"I am taking him to Colonel Bouquet. If you want one, there are plenty of them running yonder in the woods, and you may catch one for yourself," replied the Highlander.

The officer drew his pistol and shot the prisoner through the head, which cowardly deed greatly incensed the brave Highlander and called forth the indignant rebuke of Bouquet, when informed of the affair.

Sixty dead Indians were found on the field, and many wounded had been conveyed away by their friends. Bouquet had won a decisive but dearly bought victory. Eight officers were killed or severely wounded, and in all one hundred and fifteen men, or nearly one-fourth of the entire force had been killed, wounded or were missing, as a result of the two day's conflict.

The pack horse drivers emerged from the bushes, and, in company with some of the Rangers, proceeded to scalp the dead Indians, whom the regular troops disdained to touch.

So many of the horses had escaped through their neglect and cowardice during the conflict that a large quantity of valuable stores had to be destroyed for lack of transportation to prevent them from falling into the hands of the Indians after the army passed on. Litters were made and the wounded were borne to Bushy Run, where the army encamped to rest and refresh themselves after the exhausting struggle of the past two days. After the severe handling they had lately received it was supposed the Indians would not molest them soon again. But scarcely had they gone into camp before a volley was fired into their midst. The angered Highlanders soon dispersed the prowling miscreants without awaiting orders to do so. Ten of the wounded died at Bushy Run and were buried next day where Harrison City now stands. The Indians returned to the battlefield after night and scalped all the dead they could find. These gory trophies they shook at the garrison and raised the scalp haloo, as they marched past Fort Pitt in a body, a short time before the army appeared on the morning of Aug. 10.

As on the night before, Bouquet rested not until he had written his report of the day's conflict, which was done in such a complete manner that he never had occasion to change or supplement it.

Through the courtesy of her Majesty's government I have been furnished with an authentic copy of Bouquet's reports of these conflicts. The official reports are in all respects the same as given by Parkman, except the indicated omission by the copyist of the scalping operations of the Rangers and packhorse drivers, which I have supplied from Parkman's full text. But the detailed tabular statement of killed, wounded and missing in the Bushy Run battles I have never seen published elsewhere, not even by Parkman.

It is very important and interesting, showing the relative losses of the Highlanders, Royal Americans and Rangers. The first named formed nearly two-thirds of Bouquet's force, and besides having to do the heavy work, making repeated bayonet charges, they were not used to the Indian's mode of fighting as were the small detachments of Rangers and Royal Americans. Hence the loss of the gallant Scotch far exceeds that of all other parties combined. The 42nd Regiment of Royal Highlanders bore the brunt of the fierce assaults in front in the first day's battle and has a proud record on the roll of honour.

# Bouquets' Report of Second Day's Fight

Camp at Bushy Run,
6th Aug. 1763.

Sir: I had the honour to inform your Excellency in my letter of yesterday of our first engagement with the savages.

We took the post last night on the hill where our convoy halted, when the front was attacked, (a commodious piece of ground and just spacious enough for our purpose). There we encircled the whole and covered our wounded with flour bags.

In the morning the savages surrounded our camp, at the distance of 500 yards, and by shouting and yelping, quite round that extensive circumference, thought to have terrified us with their numbers. They attacked us early, and under favour of an incessant fire, made several bold efforts to penetrate our camp, and though they failed in the attempt, our situation was not the less perplexing, having experienced that brisk attacks had little effect upon an enemy who always gave way when pressed, and appeared again immediately. Our troops were, besides, extremely fatigued with the long march and as long action of the preceding day, and distressed to the last degree, by a total want of water, much more intolerable than the enemy's fire.

Tied to our convoy, we could not lose sight of it without exposing it and our wounded to fall a prey to the savages, who pressed upon us, on every side, and to move it was impracticable, having lost many horses, and most of the drivers, stupefied by fear, hid themselves in the bushes, or were incapable of hearing or obeying orders. The savages growing every moment more audacious, it was thought proper to still increase their confidence by that means, if possible, to entice them to come close upon us, or to stand their ground when attacked.

With this view two companies of Light Infantry where ordered within the circle and the troops on their right and left opened their files and filled up the space, that it might seem they were intended to cover the retreat. The Third Light Infantry company and the Grenadiers of the 42nd were ordered to support the two first companies. This manoeuvre succeeded to our wish, for the few troops who took possession of the ground lately occupied by the two Light Infantry companies being brought in nearer to the centre of the circle, the barbarians mistaking these motions for a retreat, hurried headlong on, and advancing upon us, with the most daring intrepidity, galled us excessively with their heavy fire; but at the very moment that they felt certain of success, and thought themselves masters of the camp, Major Campbell, at the head of the first companies, sallied out from a part of the hill they could not observe, and fell upon their right flank. They resolutely returned the fire but could not stand the irresistible shock of our men, who, rushing in among them, killed many of them and put the rest to flight. The orders sent to the other two companies were delivered so timely by Captain Basset, and executed with such celerity and spirit, that the routed savages who happened that moment to run before their front, received their full fire, when uncovered by the trees. The four companies did not give them time to load a second time, nor even to look behind them, but pursued them till they were totally dispersed in. The left of the savages, which had not been attacked, were kept in awe by the remains of our troops, posted on the brow of the hill for that purpose; nor durst they attempt to support or assist their right, but being witness to their defeat, followed their example and fled. Our brave men disdained so much as to touch the dead body of a vanquished enemy that scarce a scalp was taken except by the Rangers and packhorse drivers.

The woods being now cleared and the pursuit over, the four companies took possession of a hill in our front, and as soon as litters could be made for the wounded, and the flour and everything destroyed, which, for want of horses, could not be carried, we marched without molestation to this camp. After the severe correction we had given the savages a few hours before, it was natural to suppose we should enjoy some rest, but we had hardly fixed our camp, when they fired upon us again. This was very provoking; however, the Light Infantry dispersed them before they could receive orders for that purpose. I hope we shall be no more disturbed, for, if we have another action, we shall hardly be able to carry our wounded.

The behaviour of the troops on this occasion, speaks for itself so strongly, that for me to attempt their eulogium would but detract from their merit.

    I have the honour to be, most respectfully, Sir, &c.

Henry Bouquet,

To His Excellency, Sir Jeffery Amherst.

P. S.—I have the honour to enclose the return of the killed, wounded and missing in the two engagements.

H. B.

(COLONIAL CORRESPONDENCE—AMERICAN AND WEST INDIES—SIR JEFF. AMHERST, 1763, VOL. 97.)

New York, 3rd Sept., 1763.

My Lord:—On the 10th of last month Colonel Bouquet got his convoy into Fort Pitt, after having been attacked, on the 5th and 6th by a very numerous body of savages, which he repulsed and defeated, though not without some loss on our side. Captain Lieutenant Graham and Lieutenant James McIntosh, of the 42nd, being killed, with an officer of Rangers, and four officers wounded—in the whole, forty-nine were killed and sixty wounded. As I have the honour to transmit to your Lordship Colonel Bouquet's letter with my answers, and the account I made public here of that affair, I need not repeat the praises due to the troops for their behaviour, clogged as they were by a large but necessary convoy, and on a very untoward communication.

I have honour to be with the utmost respect, my Lord, your Lordship's most humble and obedient servant,

Jeffery Amherst.

Right honourable Earl of Egremont.

The copies of Colonel Henry Bouquet's official reports of the battles with the Indians, near Bushy Run, I have received direct from the British government, in response to a letter written last January, which was endorsed by Hon. Wm. S. Stenger, Secretary of Commonwealth; Hon. H. P. Laird, General R. C. Drum, Secretary of War Lincoln, and transmitted officially by Secretary of State Frelinghuysen.

The reports of Bouquet, written in the midst of such exciting and confusing scenes are models of exactness and reflect high honour upon him as a soldier and a scholar. Although a Swiss and well acquainted with German, French and other European languages, he wrote English better than the great majority of English officers.

With the aid of these reports and Hutchins' map, drawn up a few years after the battle, it is easy to locate the field of conflict. The first day's fight, where the 42nd Highland regiment suffered so severely, took place on the Gonaware Hills, near Harrison City, located on Bushy Run. The fight around the convoy, where the savages were finally ambushed and routed, took place on the Wanamaker farm, a short distance south-east of Mr. W.'s present residence. The old Forbes road ran through the Wanamaker and Gongaware farms, along a different line from the present road, but that line is well known by Mr. W., and others, who cleared away the native woods on both sides of the Forbes road. By comparing the march and resources of Bouquet with those of other Indian fighters, we are filled with increasing admiration at his success, August 5 and 6, 1763, on the bloody fields near Bushy Run.

With a force of less than 500 men, mostly composed of raw Highlanders unused to Indian warfare, Bouquet defended his convoy of 340 packhorses and finally routed the horde of savages who had fought with unusual courage and sagacity. True, he lost about one-fourth of his men in killed and wounded, but an equal or greater loss was inflicted on his wily and savage foes. Compare this with the results of similar conflicts. Braddock, in 1755, with 1,400 men, lost nearly 900, and out of 85 officers, 64 were killed or wounded. And yet he was opposed by only a few hundred Indians and French, who lost only thirty, all told, of their number. As a consequence, the borders were desolated for hundreds of miles and thousands of pioneers were driven from their homes or massacred.

Colonel Crawford, with 500 men, in 1782, was routed, and himself, his son and son-in-law captured and burned at the stake.

Colonel Loughrey, with 140 picked frontiersmen from Westmoreland, was surprised and all his force captured by an Indian detachment in 1781.

General Harmer, 1790, with 300 regulars and over 1,000 volunteers was routed with a loss of several hundred of his best troops.

General St. Clair, a brave and able officer, 1791, with 1,200 men, in line of battle, expecting attack and provided with artillery, and with large reinforcements near at hand, met with overwhelming defeat, and a loss of 68 officers killed 28 wounded, together with over half of his men. And these were for the most part veterans, used to fighting and commanded by gallant and experienced officers.

In the light of these and many similar conflicts in the olden times or in recent years, the valour and ability of Bouquet shine forth in resplendent colours. Or take a successful Indian fighter like General Anthony Wayne and we find that Bouquet stands the peer of the greatest. General Wayne had over 1,500 veteran and mounted Kentuckians and 2,000 regulars, including artillery in 1794. After sharp fighting, he routed about half his number of Indians, with a loss of thirty-three killed and a hundred of his own men wounded. The loss of the Indians was about the same as that of the whites. Under Braddock's management the Indians killed fifty white to every one of their own number slain, while under Bouquet's management they lost more of their own warriors than they were able to destroy of the whites. It is to honour the memory and perpetuate the heroism of this superb man and his gallant army of deliverance that Westmorelanders and all patriotic citizens of West Pennsylvania, Virginia and Ohio are invited to assemble on the historic field of his grandest triumph, Aug. 6, 1003.

Parkman the historian of Colonial times says:

> The Battle of Bushy Run was one of the best contested actions ever fought between white men and Indians. The Indians displayed throughout a fierceness and intrepidity matched only by the steady valour with which they were met. In the provinces the victory excited equal joy and admiration, especially among those who knew the incalculable difficulties of an Indian campaign. The Assembly of Pennsylvania passed a vote expressing their sense of the merits of Bouquet and of the services he had rendered to the province. He soon after received the additional honour of the formal thanks of the king.

The army in a few days reached Fort Pitt, to the great joy and relief of the garrison, whose stock of provisions were about exhausted. Bouquet wrote, as follows:

> To Sir Jeffery Amherst:
> Fort Pitt, Aug. 11. 1763.
> Sir:—We arrived here yesterday without further opposition than scattered shots along the road.
> The Delawares, Shawanees, Wiandots and Mingoes, had closely beset and attacked this fort from the 27th July to the 1st inst., when they quitted it to march against us.

The boldness of those savages is hardly credible; they had taken post under the banks of both rivers close to the fort, where digging holes, they kept an incessant fire, and threw fire arrows. They are good marksmen, and though our people were under cover, they killed one and wounded seven. Captain Ecuyer is wounded in the leg by an arrow. I should not do justice to that officer should I omit mentioning, that without engineer or any other artificers than a few shipwrights, he has raised a parapet of logs round the fort above the old one (which, having not been finished was too low and enfiladed) palisaded the inside of the area, constructed a fire engine, and, in short, has taken all precautions, which art and judgement could suggest, for the preservation of this post, open before on three sides, which had suffered by the floods. The inhabitants have acted with spirit against the enemy, and in the repairs of the fort. Captain Ecuyer expresses an entire satisfaction in their conduct.

The artillery and the small number of regulars have done their duty with distinction.

Sir Jeffery Amherst's letters add to the above accounts, that by his last intelligence the number of savages in the two actions of the 5th and 6th of August slain, was about sixty, and a great many wounded in the pursuit. That the three principle ringleaders of those people, who had the greatest share in fomenting the present troubles and were concerned in the murder of Colonel Clapham, &c., *viz*: Kikyuscuting, and the Wolf and Butler, were, according to the information sent him, killed; the two former in the field, and the last at Fort Pitt.

# The Ownership of the Bushy Run Tract

It has been asserted by some writers, in recent as well as colonial days, that Colonel Ephraim Blaine was in command of Fort Ligonier, which he bravely defended with provincial troops until Bouquet came along, after which he accompanied the army as commander of the packhorse brigade, and took an active part in the battle of Bushy Run, where he came near losing his life, &c. He then resolved that someday he would become the owner of that historic field.

All this is pure fiction, evidently gotten up for a special purpose, in order to invalidate the claims of the Byerlys to the grant on Bushy Run, originally given by Colonel Bouquet and secured by settlement and valuable improvements.

The name and record of Lieutenant Archibald Blane, (not Blaine), who defended Fort Ligonier with a detachment of Royal Americans in 1763, have been confounded with those of Colonel Ephraim Blaine, who first appears as a commissary sergeant in Bouquet's campaign of 1764. Neither Lieutenant A. Blane nor Colonel E. Blaine was in the Bushy Run battle. The former wrote Bouquet a letter from Fort Ligonier, immediately after the battle, congratulating him on his recent victory at Bushy Run. See Parkman's *Pontiac*, Vol. 2., p. 160. See also page 407, of *Washington—Irvine correspondence*—where Ephraim Blaine's record is correctly sketched.

The truth is Ephraim Blaine jumped the older and original Byerly claim by a patent, confirmed by the Pennsylvania Executive Council in the distracted days of 1786, long after the death of the elder Byerly, and when his widow and children were in no shape to dispute his unjust usurpation. For forty-one pounds of provincial currency, when that currency was comparatively worthless, he managed to get a technical title to the old Byerly tract of over 300 acres along the Forbes road, on the historic held of Bushy Run! This was bad enough surely, but to make him one of the chief heroes in the fight, to boost up the unjust claim, is to violate not only the rights of a family but the rights of humanity. It pollutes the fountains and muddies the sacred stream of history itself.

It was no great credit to be in command of the packhorse brigade at the Bushy Run battle, as Colonel Bouquet's report indicates. And we do Colonel Blaine's memory a service by relieving him from the equivocal position in which certain prominent individuals placed him in the suit for ownership of the battlefield, when they testified that Colonel Blaine took part in the battle of 1763 as commander of me packhorse brigade, &c. Hon. Jos. H. Kuhns, who was counsel for the Blaines in the later stages of the suit, (when Blaine's friends claimed that he had bought Byerly's right and title) told the writer a few weeks ago that the general feeling at the time of the trial was that the Byerlys had right and justice on their side. The presiding judge, being a resident of Carlisle and a special friend of the Blaines, was blamed with partiality. Until recently Mr. Kuhns believed the fiction about the presence and narrow escape of Colonel Ephraim Blaine in the battle, &c., which had been palmed off in the courts, &c., at the trial.

But after learning the real facts in the case, and seeing how the names and records of Lieutenant Archibald Blane and Colonel Ephraim Blaine had been confounded, he wrote me the following candid note on the subject:

Greensburg, Pa., May 2, 1883.

Rev. Cyrus Cort:
Rev. and Dear Sir.—Your esteemed favour received. I am satisfied that the story of Blaine's claim to the battle ground is apocryphal. He was an intruder upon Byerly,

who was, in point of fact, the first actual owner of the ground by occupancy and legal authority of the proprietary government of Penn'a.

Respectfully,

Jos. H. Kuhns.

So much for the question of original and rightful ownership of Bushy Run battlefield. Byerly removed his family to Fort Bedford, by advice of Bouquet, until peace was firmly established at the end of next year. He then returned and occupied the grant on Bushy Run. About the time of the breaking out of the Revolutionary war, he took his son Andrew to Lancaster, Pa., to give him a chance to get an education at the home of his step-sisters. While on this visit the old gentleman died, and was buried at Strasburg, in that county. I am indebted to Ad. J. Eberly, Esq., and Rev. J. A. Peters for the following which should have been stated earlier under "Byerly at Bushy Run":

> *Record book B*, page 349, contains a deed from James Hamilton, Esq., to Andreas Byerly, for a lot of ground on east side of North Queen street, a frontage of 64 feet and 4½ inches and a depth of 245 feet, in the town of Lancaster, Pa., dated October 25, 1745.

The baptismal records of the First Reformed church of Lancaster, Ira., mention Andreas Byerly as standing sponsor for a child, Feb. 3, 1745. So also, on May 3, 1750, he and his wife served in same capacity for a child by name of Houck, from Strasburg Twp., and again for a Backenstopp, Feb. 4, 1753, under the pastorates of Revs. Schnorr, Vock and Otterbein, respectively.

The Byerly family resided for greater safety at Fort Walthour during the Revolution. Jacob served in several campaigns against the Indians and killed a chief in a fight near Brady's Bend, when quite a young man.

Mrs. Byerly was a very intelligent, humane and pious woman. She had been well trained in the doctrines of the Reformed Church of Switzerland. She did good service as a nurse and a kind of doctoress during those dark and dangerous days. But her care was extended to the soul as well as body. She established a

Sunday school for the intellectual and religious training of the neglected children at the fort, and in various ways was a public benefactress. Some years after Mr. Byerly's death she was married to a Mr. Lord, an Englishman. She lies buried among her children at the old Brush Creek graveyard. Andrew Byerly had four sons, *viz.*: Michael, Jacob, Francis and Andrew.

Their descendants are scattered over a great part of the United States. Jacob entered the Revolutionary army at sixteen and saw hard service for several years in helping to guard the frontiers against Indians and Tories. His son Andrew was major in the War of 1812, and guarded the ships of Commodore Perry's fleet, while being built on Lake Erie. Benjamin was a lieutenant and Joseph a private, as also his son-in-law, Skelly, in the same war. Benjamin was likewise sheriff and assemblyman.

Captain George A. Cribbs, who fell at the head of his men at the second battle of Manassas, was married to a granddaughter of Jacob Byerly, and Sergeant Cyrus Rankin, who fell on the Peninsula, was a great grandson.

Mrs. James Gregg, of Greensburg, is a granddaughter of Michael, and Daniel C. Byerly, deceased, was a grandson.

Prof. Andrew Byerly, of Millersville Normal School, is a grandson of Andrew II.

The descendants of Francis Byerly are numerous in Iowa. Michael, Jacob and Francis married three sisters named Harmon, whose mother was Christina Lenhart, from Holland. Jacob was married in old Fort Walthour, by 'Squire Trouby, during the Revolution. He and his son Joseph are buried with fine military monuments at Brush Creek graveyard.

# Evil Results of Provincial Apathy

After their discomfiture at Bushy Run, the Indians moved from their towns along the Alleghany and Ohio Rivers into the Muskingum country, where they fancied themselves entirely safe from molestation, while at the same time they could carry on their depredations by sudden incursions into the white settlements. It would have been wise policy and an immense saving of life and treasure had they been followed at once to their forest fastnesses and brought to terms by a display of military prowess in their own haunts.

This was exactly what Bouquet proposed to do. As soon as he had brought his heavy convoy through from Fort Ligonier to Fort Pitt, he made strenuous efforts to secure reinforcements for such an expedition into the heart of the Indian country.

August 27, 1763, he wrote General Amherst from Fort Pitt that with a re-enforcement of three hundred Provincial Rangers he could destroy all the Delaware towns and clear the country of that vermin between this fort and Lake Erie. He bitterly complained that the provinces would not even furnish escorts to convoys, so that his hands were completely tied. He candidly admitted the importance and value of provincials for service against the savages in the woods, something which Amherst, like Braddock before him, was loath to do.

October 24, 1763, he writes the haughty and obstinate Amherst as follows:

> Without a certain number of woodsmen, I cannot think it advisable to employ regulars in the woods against savages, as they cannot procure any intelligence and are open

to continual surprises, nor can they pursue to any distance their enemy when they have routed them; and should they have the misfortune to be defeated, the whole would be destroyed, if above one day's march from a fort. That is my opinion, in which I hope to be deceived.

The Quaker Provincial authorities, backed by the Dunkard and Mennonite elements among the Germans, seemed to be utterly insensible to the dangers and sufferings of the exposed settlements near the borders. In their more secure abodes in the older settlements they would prate about the wickedness of war and try to justify their impracticable theories by extensive scriptural quotations.

St. Paul teaches that civil government is a divine institution, and its representatives must not bear the sword in vain but be a terror to evil-doers and a praise to them that do well. See *Rom.*, 13.

All this was ignored, and in place of it was substituted a perverted theory of non-resistance. The exhortations to individual Christians to forego the gratification of private or personal revenge, on the ground of the old law of retaliation, was applied to civil rulers and governments in a way that was contrary to reason and Scripture.

The Great Cove, in Blair county, was settled by Dunkards as early as 1755. These were exposed to Indian raids. "*Gottes wille sei gethan,*" they would say, while the brutal savages were tomahawking their wives and children, in whose defence they would not lift a finger. They seemed to think that it was the Lord's will that the devil and his agents should have full swing without opposition.

The strong and vigorous Scotch Presbyterian and the German Reformed and Lutheran elements of the population had no patience or sympathy with such sentimental views. When their families or friends were being ruthlessly slaughtered by the savages, they were filled with indignation against all who either directly or indirectly abetted the cruel destroyers of life and property.

Large numbers of Reformed and Lutheran families had settled along the Codorus, the Conewago, the Monocacy and Conococheague streams of Pennsylvania and Maryland, where regularly organised congregations existed already in 1748, as we learn from the *Life and Travels of Rev. Michael Schlatter*. So also, at Winchester and other points through the Shenandoah Valley.

The Royal American Regiment, as we have seen, was largely composed of this element and commanded by experienced German and Swiss officers, who had seen service in the armies of the Dutch Republic.

The horrors of savage warfare fell upon these settlements and soldiers, together with their Scotch-Irish neighbours, in the Conococheague settlements.

The friendly Conestoga Indians in Lancaster county and the Moravian Indian converts along the Lehigh were blamed for harbouring and abetting some of the marauding Indians, and the full force of popular fury was arrayed against them. When homes were being daily desolated, parents tomahawked and scalped, and children carried into heathen captivity, it was natural for the people to hate the name of Indian and to be filled with wrath at any one who would protect or countenance any member of the race. The supineness of the Provincial Assembly, and their failure to second the efforts of such a man as Bouquet was discouraging and demoralizing and provoking in the extreme to the regular troops, who had suffered so much on the outposts, and to the hardy pioneers in the advanced settlements.

The Paxton Boys, in their riotous conduct at the Lancaster jail and in their march to Philadelphia, helped to awaken the Quakers from their dream of lethargic indifference. The Royal Americans had been kept in the woods for over six years, and now Amherst sought to compel regulars to remain in service after the long term of enlistment had expired. These causes combined to produce great discontent, both among officers and men. They were expected to hold many important posts and keep up long lines of communication in the midst of the wilderness, surrounded by prowling and hostile savages.

Lieutenant Archibald Blane and the gallant Captain Ecuyer asked Bouquet to be relieved from labours and responsibilities too heavy for their strength and resources. And Bouquet himself chagrined, at some action of the British government which seemed to shut the door of promotion against foreign born officers and worried out of patience by the ingratitude and neglect of the provinces, felt himself constrained to do the same thing.

Amherst had left for England, disgusted with the situation and angry at the provinces for want of co-operation. General Gage had taken his place as commander-in-chief. Bouquet wrote Gage, June 20, 1764, asking to be relieved of the command, the burden and fatigues of which were too great for his strength to endure much longer.

He thus refers to the condition of the troops at the same time:

> The three companies of Royal Americans were reduced, when I met them at Lancaster, to fifty-five men, having lost thirty-eight by desertion, in my short absence. I look upon Sir Jeffery Amherst's orders forbidding me to continue to discharge, as usual, the men whose term of service was expired, and keeping us seven years in the woods, as the occasion of this unprecedented desertion. The encouragement given everywhere in this country to deserters, screened almost by every person, must in time ruin the army unless the laws against harbourers are better enforced by the American (provincial) Government.

But Gage would not consent to relieve so useful a man in such an emergency. It was agreed that two strong bodies of troops should proceed into the Indian country to do what Bouquet was anxious to do the previous summer, *i.e.* chastise the savages into submission in their own native strongholds. Bradstreet was to take a large force by way of the Lakes and co-operate with Bouquet, who was to march with his Bushy Run veterans (what was left of them) and a large force of provincial rangers to be raised in Pennsylvania, Virginia and Maryland.

The Pennsylvania Assembly voted to raise three hundred men to guard the frontiers and one thousand to join Bouquet's expedition into Ohio. Virginia and Maryland at first refused to do anything for the common defence.

# Massacre of a Schoolmaster and Ten Scholars

The summer of 1764 was rapidly passing away, and nothing effective had yet been done. The Indians continued their ravages and penetrated deeper and deeper into the settlements, killing and slaying the defenceless people.

In 1764, July 26, three miles north-west of Greencastle, Franklin county, Pa., was perpetrated what Parkman, the great historian of Colonial times, pronounces 'an outrage unmatched in fiend-like atrocity through all the annals of the war.'

This was the massacre of Enoch Brown, a kind-hearted exemplary Christian schoolmaster, and ten scholars, eight boys and two girls. Ruth Hart and Ruth Hale were the names of the girls. Among the boys were Eben Taylor, George Dustan and Archie McCullough. All were knocked down like so many beeves and scalped by the merciless savages. Mourning and desolation came to many homes in the valley, for each of the slaughtered innocents belonged to a different family. The last-named boy, indeed, survived the effects of the scalping knife, but in a somewhat demented condition.

The teacher offered his life and scalp in a spirit of self-sacrificing devotion if the savages would only spare the lives of the little ones under his charge and care. But no! the tender mercies of the heathen are cruel, and so a perfect holocaust was made to the Moloch of war by the relentless fiends in human form. The school house was located on the farm now occupied by Mr. Henry Diehl, and formerly owned by Mr. Christian Koser. It stood in a cleared field, at the head of a deep ravine, surrounded by dense forests. Down this ravine the savages fled a mile or two until they struck Conococheague Creek, along the bed of which, to conceal their tracks, they travelled to the mouth of Path Valley, up which and across the mountains they made good their escape to their village, near the Ohio.

It is some relief to know that this diabolical deed, whose recital makes us shudder even at this late date, was disapproved by the old warriors when the marauding party of young Indians came back with their horrid trophies. Neephaughwhese, or Night Walker, an old chief or half-king, denounced them as a pack of cowards for killing and scalping so many children.

But who can describe the agony of those parents in the Conococheague, settlement weeping like Rachel for her children and refusing to be comforted? Or who can describe the horror of the scene in that lonely log school house, when one of the settlers chanced to look in at the door to ascertain the cause of the unusual quietness.

In the centre lay the faithful Brown, scalped and lifeless, with a Bible clasped in his hand. Around the room were strewn the dead and mangled bodies of seven boys and two girls, while little Archie, stunned, scalped and bleeding, was creeping around among his dead companions, rubbing his hands over their faces and trying to gain some token of recognition.

A few days later the innocent victims of savage atrocity received a common sepulchre. All were buried in one large, rough box at the border of the ravine, a few rods from the school house where they had been so ruthlessly slaughtered. Side by side, with head and feet alternately, the little ones were laid with their master, just as they were clad at the time of the massacre. Strange to say, no memorial tablet has ever been erected over their remains. Tradition has preserved the exact location of the common grave of master and scholars, and it is not too late yet for grateful, patriotic and philanthropic Christian people, enjoying the blessings of civilization, peace and prosperity, to render this duty of the living to the martyred dead.

August 4, 1843, or seventy-nine years after the slaughter, a number of the principal citizens of Greencastle made excavations to verify the traditional account of the place and manner of burial. Some remains of the rough coffin were found at quite a depth from the surface, and then the skull and other remains of a grown person, alongside of which were remains of several children. Metal buttons, part of a tobacco-box, teeth, &c, were picked up as relics by those present, among whom were some of our citizens still living with us in a green old age, *viz*: Dr. Wm. Grubb, Dr. J. K. Davison, Geo. W. Zeigler, Esq., and General David Detrich.

There was a good deal of talk at the time about the propriety of buying the adjacent grounds, laying out a road and erecting a monument; but nothing definite was ever done. Mr. Koser, the owner of the farm, took a lively interest in the matter, and in lieu of a better memorial planted four locust trees to mark the corners of the grave. Two of these only survived and are mentioned by S. H. Eby, Esq., Superintendent of Common Schools, in his interesting report, published 1877. But, alas! even these imperfect historic landmarks were cut down a few years ago for the sake of making a few posts, and Mr. Koser's well-meant efforts to preserve the identity of the grave have thus in a measure been thwarted. The stumps remain as frail indices by which the exact location of the grave may still be accurately determined.

Such is the present state of the case as ascertained last Wednesday (April 11, 1883), on a visit to the spot by General David Detrich, Colonel B. F. Winger and Rev. Cyrus Cort.

The foregoing is an extract from an article that appeared in the *Greencastle Press*.

> I am glad to be able to report that as a result of the visit just mentioned, steps having been taken by public spirited citizens of Greencastle to have the grave of Brown and his martyred scholars duly marked by a permanent monument at an early day.

Atrocities like these helped to arouse the slumbering provinces to the necessity of bold and energetic measures.

# Campaign of 1764

On the 5th of August the two Pennsylvania battalions under Lieutenant Colonels Francis and Clayton were assembled at Carlisle. Governor Penn had come up from Philadelphia with Colonel Bouquet and addressed the troops. He spoke of the necessity of chastising the Indians:

> For their repeated and unprovoked barbarities on the inhabitants of the Province, a just resentment of which added to a remembrance of the loyalty and courage of our provincial troops on former occasions he did not doubt, would animate them to do honour to their country, and that they could not but hope to be crowned with success as they were to be united with the same regular troops and under the same able commander who had by themselves on that very day, the memorable 5th of August, in the preceding year, sustained the repeated attacks of the savages and obtained a complete victory over them.

Governor Penn also reminded them of the exemplary punishments that would be inflicted on the grievous crime of desertion, if any of them were capable of so far forgetting their solemn oath and duty to their king and country as to be involved in it. Colonel Bouquet then took command of the troops, regular and provincial. After four days of necessary preparation for the long march, the army set out.

Colonel Bouquet gave very strict "orders to officers and men to observe strict discipline and not to commit the least violation of the civil rights or peace of the inhabitants."

His care and conduct in this respect stand forth in happy contrast with that of many militia or emergency men who came up the valley to defend the borders from invasion a hundred years later, but who in the end were more harmful and more dreaded by the loyal people of the borders than the disciplined host of Southern invaders under Lee.

# Desertions of Provincial Troops

In spite of all precautions, no less than 200 desertions took place by August 13, when the army reached Fort Londoun.

Bouquet asked permission to fill up the contingent, which was granted by resolution of the governor and commissioners August 16. He then applied to Colonel Lewis for 200 Virginia volunteers, to take the place of the deserters. With the co-operation of Governor Fauquier the men were soon raised and joined Bouquet at Fort Pitt in the latter part of September.

These Virginia volunteer riflemen were among his best troops, but in the end, Virginia ungratefully left Colonel Bouquet in the lurch as regards their payment.

At Fort Loudoun, Bouquet received a very presumptuous and characteristic letter from Colonel Bradstreet, telling him that he need not proceed any farther, inasmuch as peace had been concluded with the Delawares and Shawanees. At that very time these same tribes were scalping settlers in all directions. Bradstreet was ambitious to gain all the glory of the campaign.

Instead of minding his own business and compelling the Lake Indians to bring in their captives and give proper guarantees of sub-mission, he turned aside in his course to attend to the business assigned to Bouquet, who was his superior officer. As the whole scheme was a ruse on the part of the Ohio Indians to gain time and prevent Bouquet's advance, he and General Gage were both indignant at Bradstreet and repudiated his officious intermeddling.

Without delaying an hour, Bouquet pushed forward. September 5, he had reached Fort Bedford, where more Pennsylvanians deserted, taking along their arms and horses. A large reinforcement of friendly Indians, promised to be sent from the Six Nations by Sir. Wm. Johnson, never arrived. At Ligonier he received from General Gage the hearty endorsement of his own conduct, and the repudiation of Bradstreet's unwarranted and premature negotiations with irresponsible representatives of the Ohio Indians.

# Arrival at Fort Pitt

He passed safely over the historic field of Bushy Run to Fort Pitt, where he was rejoiced to receive the Virginia reinforcement. Ten Indians came to the opposite bank of the river, proposing a conference. Finding that they were evidently spies, endeavouring to gain important information, he detained two of them as hostages, and sent another one with two messengers to Bradstreet and a statement to the Ohio Indians that if any harm was done to these two men, the Indian hostages in his hands should be put to death at once and dire vengeance executed against their entire nation.

Several Iroquois Indians came into the fort, pretending great friendship, and assuring him that the Ohio Indians would speedily return all the white captives. They spoke of the difficulty of penetrating the hilly forests and the great numbers of the Indians who would oppose the army, but who would soon fulfil all his stipulations if he only remained quietly at Fort Pitt. The whole object of these crafty envoys was evidently to delay the campaign until bad weather and lateness of the season made it impossible.

Bouquet saw through their designs and sent them to tell the Delawares and Shawanees, &c., that he was on his way to punish their cruel and perfidious conduct unless they made prompt and complete submission to his terms.

# The March into Ohio

Early in October the army left Fort Pitt to cut a road directly through the unexplored wilderness of Ohio. The Colonel assured the troops of his confidence in their bravery and told them that he did not doubt but that this war would soon be ended, under God, to their own honour and the future safety of their country, provided the men were strictly obedient to orders and guarded against the surprises and sudden attacks of a treacherous enemy, who never dared to face British troops in an open held.

Large droves of sheep and cattle were taken along for subsistence, besides great droves of packhorses loaded with flour and other provisions. The Virginia woodsmen acted as scouts and flankers in front and on the sides, whilst the pioneers cleared the road through the dense forest. The army, with flocks and herds and camp equipage, followed the pioneers at the rate of seven or eight miles a day, moving constantly in a series of concentric hollow squares, with hocks, herds, baggage, packhorses, &c. in the centre.

Thus, in line of battle and guarding carefully against ambush and surprise, they moved steadily forward. Skulking Indians were watching every movement, but no direct attempt was made to interfere with the progress of the troops. The strictest discipline was enforced. Before leaving Fort Pitt two soldiers had been shot for desertion, and all superfluous women ordered back to the settlements. One woman was allowed to each corps, and two nurses for the general hospital. These were needed to look after the children and female captives, whose recovery was one chief object of the expedition. In ten days the army reached, the

Muskingum, and was now in the heart of the Indian country. Near the fording of that river, they saw the wigwams of a hundred families of Tuscarora Indians who had fled in terror at their approach. The two soldiers sent to Bradstreet, now appeared, having been detained by the Delawares on trifling pretexts until they saw the invasion was an overwhelming success. They brought word that the chiefs would come in a few days to hold a conference.

# Council on the Muskingum—Captives Restored

Bouquet marched along the Muskingum until he found ample forage in the broad meadows for his cattle, sheep and packhorses; he erected a palisaded depot for provisions and baggage. Soon a number of chiefs appeared, stating that great numbers of warriors were eight miles distant, and that a place and time should be appointed for council. He designated a spot near the river bank where he would meet them next day. A party of woodsmen soon prepared a rustic arbour, where English officers and Indian chiefs might meet under shelter. Every precaution was used to prevent a surprise or attack. Guards were doubled and no straggling allowed. The soldiers were drawn up so as to make the most stunning impression upon the minds of the savages. And truly it was a wonderful sight to see such a vast body of troops fully equipped in the midst of the wilderness, with flocks and herds, and other resources needed for a protracted campaign. The scene was as picturesque as it was astounding in its display of military prowess.

The Highland grenadiers were there with their plaids, kilts and tartans, whom the Indians styled, petticoat warriors on account of their queer dress. The Royal Americans were on hand with their bright red British uniforms, the duller garb and duller trappings of Pennsylvania troops and the fringed hunting frocks of the Virginia backwoods riflemen made such a combination of military pomp and power as has been rarely seen in any land.

The chiefs came at the appointed hour—Kiashuta, or

Guyashuta, the chief of a band of Senecas, Custaloga, chief of the Delawares, Keisnauchtha, chief of the Shawanees, each with a band of warriors, were the leaders along with Turtle Heart, Beaver, &c, they tried to frame excuses for their treacherous conduct, blaming it on the rashness of their young men and the western tribes led in person by Pontiac, they begged for peace and promised to return to him all white prisoners in their hands.

Bouquet thoroughly understood the Indian character and knew what demean or and tactics suited the occasion. He told them to return next day to receive his answer. Inclement weather prevented their proposed meeting until the twentieth. Instead of calling them brothers he began: "*Sachems*, War chiefs and Warriors." He then addressed them with great spirit, and in severe and impassioned language. He pointed out the absurdity of their trifling excuses and reminded them of their unparalleled treachery and cruelty in plundering traders and settlers, capturing children and in assaulting the king's troops in the woods at Bushy Run, last summer. He denounced their continued murderous forays upon the border settlements and condemned their repeated failures to bring back the white prisoners in their hands. He will not be deceived longer by their false promises.

He said:

> If it were possible that you could convince us that you sincerely repent of your past perfidy, and that we could depend on your good behaviour for the future, you might yet hope for mercy and peace. If I and that you faithfully execute the following preliminary conditions, I will not treat you with the severity you deserve. I give you twelve days from this date to deliver into my hands at Waukatamake, all prisoners in your possession without any exception, Englishmen, Frenchmen, women, children, whether adopted in your tribes, married or living amongst you under any denomination and pretence whatsoever, together with all negroes. And you are to furnish the said prisoners with clothing, provisions and horses to carry them to Fort Pitt. When you have fully complied with these conditions, you shall then know on what terms you may obtain the

peace you sue for.

Bouquet was as wise and sagacious as he was brave and generous. The manner as well as the sentiments of his address made a deep and lasting impression upon the supplicating savages. Their haughty spirit was completely humbled.

They abjectly promised to comply fully with all the conditions. The Delawares had already delivered up eighteen prisoners. They handed over eighty-three small sticks indicating the remaining number of prisoners in their hands, whom they promised to bring in as soon as possible. The Shawanees failed to respond properly to the Colonel's wishes, either by appearing at the council with their kings or by bringing in the captives in their hands. A sharp message was sent to them not to trifle with the patience of the commander. The army marched some thirty odd miles further to the Forks of the Muskingum, where it was agreed to await the prisoners instead of at Waukatamake.

The principal chiefs of each tribe he kept in his possession as hostages to secure the fulfilment of pledges. Great care had to be taken to prevent a general stampede of the tribes and the murder of all the prisoners in their hands as well as to secure a full compliance with the conditions of restoration. Bouquet's management inspired them with confidence and respect, while at the same time it filled them with terror and brought them into complete submission to his commands. Runners were sent out in all directions, and soon several hundred captives were brought into camp. Among these were ninety Virginians, of whom thirty-two were adult males and the rest were women and children; one hundred and sixteen Pennsylvanians, forty-nine men and sixty-seven women and children were also returned. Many of the volunteers had wives, children and relatives among the captives, and the scenes that took place at the recovery and recognition of the long lost loved ones were touching in the extreme.

With great sorrow and reluctance, the Indians parted with these adopted members of their households. For, be it remembered, that when once an Indian had adopted a captive, the captive was henceforth treated as a member of the family and not as a slave. The captive women were, as a rule, absolutely free from insult and were not even obliged to marry against their will. The reverse of this is the case among many of the Western and South-western tribes of Indians at the present day, who treat their captives as slaves and always outrage the women.

Many of the Shawanees warriors were absent on hunting expeditions, so that nearly a hundred captives could not be reached. Hostages were given for the safe delivery of these at Fort Pitt. Bouquet maintained a stern and indignant demeanour until all conditions were fulfilled as far as possible, knowing that any other deportment under circumstances would be mistaken for timidity and indecision. Kindness can only be appreciated by a savage when he knows you have ability to overwhelm him if refractory. Having fully convinced them of his prowess and displeasure at everything like duplicity, Bouquet convened the chiefs in the rustic council house again and intimated his satisfaction with their conduct and his desire to arrange for a lasting peace.

Guyasutha, the celebrated Seneca chief, who had been the leading spirit of the eastern wing of Pontiac's conspiracy, and had led the forces around Fort Pitt and at Bushy Run, made the opening speech in the metaphorical and eloquent language so characteristic of Indian orators.

Addressing Colonel Bouquet he said:

> Brother, with this string of *wampum* I dispel the thick cloud that has hung so long over our heads, that the sunshine of peace may once more descend to warm and gladden. I wipe the tears from your eyes and condole with you on the loss of your brethren who have perished in this war. I gather their bones together and cover them deep in the earth, that the sight of them may no longer bring sorrow to your hearts, and I scatter dry leaves over the spot, that it may depart forever from memory. The path of peace, which once ran between your dwellings and mine, has of late been choked with thorns and briars, so that no one could pass that way, and we have both forgotten that such a path had ever been. I now clear away all such obstructions and make a broad, smooth road, so that you and I

may freely visit each other as our fathers used to do. I kindle a great council fire whose smoke shall rise to heaven in view of all the nations while you and I sit together and smoke the peace pipe at its blaze.

The orators of each tribe spoke in similar strain promising to lay down their arms and live hereafter in peace with the English. Bouquet replied to each and all as follows:

By your full compliance with the conditions which I imposed you have satisfied me of your sincerity and I now receive you as brethren. The King, my master, has commissioned me, not to make treaties but to fight his battles; and though I now offer you peace it is not in my power to settle its precise terms and conditions. For this I refer you to Sir William Johnson, his Majesty's agent and superintendent for Indian affairs, who will settle with you the articles of peace and determine everything in relation to trade. Two things, however, I shall insist on. And first you are to give hostages as security that you will preserve good faith and send without delay a deputation of your chiefs to Sir William Johnson. In the next place these chiefs are to be fully empowered to treat in behalf of your nation; and you will bind yourselves to adhere strictly to everything they shall agree upon in your behalf.

These conditions were readily complied with, and chiefs duly designated for the mission to Sir William.

And now having gained all his points, Bouquet to the great joy and relief of the Indians extended for the first time the hand of friendship, which hitherto he had resolutely refused to do.

Nettowhatways, the chief of the Turtle tribe, having failed to co-operate properly in the peace measures, Colonel Bouquet deposed him and directed his tribe to elect another chief and present him as their proper representative, which was done a few days later.

Nov. 12, Red Hawk, Nimwha, Lavissimo, Bennevissico, and other leading Shawnees chiefs made their submission. Red Hawk instead of proposing in usual Indian style to bury the hatchet (which might in that case be dug up again) said that they as younger brothers would take it out of the hands of their older white brothers and "throw it up to God" that they might never see it again.

He then produced copies of treaties made in 1701 as an evidence of the friendly relations of their ancestors. He promised that the remainder of the prisoners would be brought into Fort Pitt in the spring which pledge was kept. Many of the captives had become so fond of Indian life that it was with difficulty that they could be induced to return to Christian homes. McCullough, one of the captives in his narrative says that Rhoda Boyd and Elizabeth Studibaker escaped from the whites and went back to the Indians. Mary Jemison, who had married among them, fled with her half-breed children and hid until the troops left the country.

This would, indicate that after their adoption captives was as a rule treated kindly and as members of their own families by their Indian captors.

One of the Virginia volunteers had lost his wife and a child, two years old, in an Indian foray into the settlement six months before. What transports filled their hearts when he met her with a babe, three months old, at her breast! Quickly he took her to his tent and furnished suitable clothing for her and her babe. But what had become of the two-year-old darling captured with its mother? She could not tell, except that it had been separated from her and taken elsewhere after their captivity.

A few days later a child was brought, in which was supposed to be the one in question. The mother was sent for, and at first was not certain that it was her child, but after carefully scrutinizing it she recognized its features, and was so overcome with joy that she dropped her young babe and, catching up the newly found child, she clasped it to her heart, and with a flood of tears carried it off. The father, picking up the child that she had let fall, followed his overjoyed wife and thus again the family circle was unbroken. The rough soldiers, and even the stolid savages were moved to feelings of sympathetic tenderness by such touches of human nature, which make the whole world of mankind akin.

November 18, the army set out for Fort Pitt, followed by many affectionate Indians, who sought to help the captives along in their homeward journey. In ten days the fort was reached just in time to escape severe winter weather. The regular troops (Highlanders and Royal Americans), were placed at the different forts and posts on the line of communication, while the volunteers returned with the captives to the provinces. Those captives, whose friends had not been able to go with the army, were taken to Carlisle, where many persons who had lost children by the Indians, flocked to discover, if possible, their captured kindred.

One German woman, from East Pennsylvania, came in search of a daughter, who had been carried off nine years before. She identified one of the young female captives as her long-lost child but could gain no token of recognition in response to her loving entreaties. The old lady lamented that the child that she had often sung to sleep on her knee had forgotten her in her old age. Bouquet, like a man of sense and humane instincts, told the woman to sing one of the songs or hymns that she used to sing to her when a child. Mrs. Hartman, the mother, obeyed as best she could, singing part of a very appropriate German hymn, of which I will give several verses, together with a translation by Rev. Samuel R. Fisher, D. D., deceased.

*Allein und doch nicht gantz alleine*
*Bin ich in meiner einsamkeit,*
*Dann wann ich gantz verlassen scheine,*
*Vertreibt mir Jesus selbst die zeit.*
*Ich bin bey Ihm, und Er bey mir,*
*So kommt nun gar nich einsam für.*
Alone and yet not all alone
Am I, in solitude though drear,
For when no one seems me to own
My Jesus will himself be near.
I am with Him and He with me,
I, therefore, cannot lonely be.
*Komm ich zur welt; man redt von sachen,*
*So nur auf eitlekeit gericht;*
*Da muss sich lassen das verlachen,*

*Der etwas von den Himmel spricht.*
*Drum wunsh ich lieber gantz allein,*
*Als bey der welt ohn Gott zu seyn.*
Seek I the world? Of things they speak,
Which are on vanity intent;
Here he is scorned and spurned as weak
Whose mind on heavenly things is bent.
I rather would my lone way plod,
Than share the world without my God.
*Verkehrte konnen leicht verkehren,*
*Wer greifet pech ohn kleben an?*
*Wie solt ich dann dahin begehren,*
*Wo man Gott bald vergessen kann?*
*Gesellschaft, die verdachtig sheint,*
*Wird ofters nach dein fall beweint.*
With ease do perverts perverts make;
Who handles pitch his hands will soil;
Why then should I with those partake,
Who of His honour God despoil?
Society which we suspect,
We often afterwards reject.
*Wer wolte dann nun recht erkennen,*
*Das ich stets in gesellschaft bin?*
*Und will die welt mich einsam nennen,*
*So thun sie es nur immerhin.*
*G'nug, dass bey mir, wann ich allein,*
*Gott und viel tausend engel seyn.*
Who will not then with candour own,
I have companions all I crave?
And will the world still deem me lone?
Then let it thus forever rave.
Enough! I've God and angels' host,
Whose number can its thousands boast.

The sweet accents of her German childhood, fell upon her enraptured ears like the song of angels, and with a gaze of fond recognition, and a passionate flood of tears, the long-lost daughter rushed into the outstretched arms of her devoted mother.

Scenes like this threw a halo of religious romance around the expedition of Bouquet. Rev. Ruben Weiser has drawn out the story of Regina Hartman, the German captive, with confessedly large drafts upon the imagination. He draws Conrad Weiser into the drama, although the great Indian interpreter had already been dead four years This is not more absurd than to foist in a German hostler to interpret between Mrs. Hartman and Colonel Bouquet, who was well acquainted with German, French, &c, or his efforts to make Regina pass through a certain religious process.

Peace and tranquillity were restored to the borders without bloodshed, and hundreds of captives were brought back from heathen bondage to blessings of Christian homes and civilization. Bouquet was the hero of the hour. Early in January 1765, he arrived in Philadelphia. The people and authorities everywhere vied with each other in expressing their highest esteem for his character, and grateful recognition of his services. The friends and relatives especially of recovered captives were filled with affectionate and reverent admiration.

# Public Thanks to Bouquet

January 15, 1765, the Assembly of Pennsylvania at its first setting, adopted a congratulatory and complimentary address, heartily thanking him for his great service to that province, by his victory at Bushy Run, Aug, 6, 1763, his recent campaign against the Ohio Indians, during which he had laid the foundation of lasting peace and rescued hundreds of Christian brethren from savage captivity; and, finally, they thanked him for his "constant attention to the civil rights of his Majesty's subjects in this province."

In like manner the House of Burgesses for the Colony and Dominion of Virginia, thanked Bouquet for his invaluable services in subduing the Indians, and recovering so many of their people from captivity.

They further requested the Governor to recommend Bouquet to the ministers of King George, as an officer of distinguished merit, in this and every former service in which he had been engaged. The gallant and chivalric colonel replied in grateful acknowledgement and generously awarded much of the credit of the success of his recent campaign to the efficiency of the provincial troops, and especially commended Colonel Lewis for his zeal and good conduct during the campaign. Colonel Reid, who was second in command, also received honourable mention from him as well as all officers, regular and provincial, who served in the expedition.

# Injustice and Ingratitude of Virginia

But every sweet has its bitter, and the oft-told tale of ingratitude and injustice to benefactors must, alas, be repeated. Virginia was lavish in her praises, as well she might be, for she had profited greatly by the campaign; but when it came to foot the bill of expenses for her small body of splendid troops during the campaign, she repudiated the obligation! "Tell it not in Gath, publish it not in the streets of Askelon!" Pontiac, the heathen savage, put such conduct to shame by scrupulously redeeming every piece of birch bark currency issued in his name for supplies during the siege of Detroit.

At length, after great personal annoyance and embarrassment, Bouquet induced the Pennsylvania Assembly to pay the Virginia troops for services and expenses incurred during the campaign of 1764.

By so doing Pennsylvania in some degree atoned for a multitude of past sins of neglect and indifference. But Bouquet was stung to the quick by the conduct of the Virginians and begs General Gage to relieve him from his present command in order that he might make a trip to Europe. His request was granted. He wrote to Gage March 4, 1765:

> The disgust I have conceived from the ill-nature and ingratitude of those individuals (the Virginia officials) makes me accept with great satisfaction your offer to discharge me of this department, in which I never desire to serve again, nor, indeed, to be commanding officer in any other, since the new regulations you were pleased to communi-

cate to me; being sensible of my inability to carry on the service upon the terms prescribed.

This had reference to some rigid prescriptions which he supposed fully closed the door against the promotion of foreign born officers.

He seems to have intended to return and settle in the provinces, or remove obstacles in the line of promotion, for the day before writing the above letter to Gage, *i.e.*, March 3, 1765, he was naturalized by the Supreme Court of Pennsylvania, in accordance with a late act of Parliament.

## Bouquet's Promotion

And now to his great surprise and the gratification of all good men, Bouquet receives tidings that the king had promoted him to the rank of brigadier general.

April 15, 1765, he wrote his grateful acknowledgement of the unexpected honour, which also gave assurance of preferment to other deserving foreign-born officers, who were among the most devoted subjects of the King. Letters of congratulation came pouring in, especially from officers who had served under him.

Captain George Etherigton, of the first battalion of Royal Americans, who so narrowly escaped massacre at Michillmackinac in May, 1763, wrote Bouquet as follows from Lancaster, Pa., April 19, 1765:

> Sir, though I almost despair of this reaching you before you sail to Europe, yet I cannot deny myself the pleasure of giving you joy on your promotion, and can, with truth, tell you that it gives great joy to all the gentlemen of the battalion, for two reasons: first, on your account; and secondly, on our own, as by that means we may hope for the pleasure of continuing under your command. You can hardly imagine how this place rings with the news of your promotion, for the townspeople and German farmers stop us in the street to ask if it is true that the king has made Colonel Bouquet a general; and when they are told it is true, they march off with great joy; so, you see the old proverb wrong for once, which says he that prospers is

envied; for sure I am that all the people are more pleased with the news of your promotion than they would be if the government would take off the stamp duty.

Dr. Wm. Smith, Provost of the University and historian of his campaigns, spoke the common sentiment when he said Bouquet had become "as dear by his private virtues to those who have the honour of his more intimate acquaintance as he is by his military service to the public." For this reason:

> It is hoped he may long continue among us, where his experienced abilities will enable him, and his love of the English constitution entitle him, to fill any future trust to which His Majesty may be pleased to call him.

It had been Bouquet's hope and desire to visit England and to return again to the scenes of his earlier career among the Lowlands of Holland and the mountains of Switzerland, but the king assigned him to the command of the Southern military department, and as the Indians had recently become troublesome in that locality, he repaired to his new field of action without unnecessary delay.

# Leaves for Pensacola Will and Death

Before leaving Philadelphia, he made his last will and testament, which I copied a few weeks ago at the office of the Register of Wills, in Philadelphia. It is in his own handwriting, and reads thus:

> In the name of God, Amen. I, Henry Bouquet, Brigadier General of his Majesty's forces, serving in North America, have thought fit to dispose of my estate, real and personal, after my death, in the following manner: I give and bequeath for the use of the hospital of Pennsylvania, forty pounds of that currency. I give and bequeath to my friend, Thos. Willing, Esq., five tracts of land of two hundred acres each, surveyed or to be surveyed for me in Trough Creek Valley, by virtue of the warrants granted me at the land office, and now to the amount of thirteen, including one to be given by Geo. Croghan, Esq., in the hands of Mr. Robert Callendar, living near Carlisle, in Cumberland county; amounting in the whole to two thousand eight hundred acres, for which I paid only the warrant money.
> I give and bequeath to John Schneider, the boy who is bound to me, the sum of fifty pounds currency to be paid him when he is of age by Colonel Haldimand, to whom I recommend my other servants. All my just debts are to be paid, consisting at present in one thousand pounds sterling, besides interests to Mr. G. Heneman, solicitor of the Swiss troops at The Hague in Holland—in my note in hand to account current with Mr. Adam Hoops, the note

being for two hundred and fifty pounds being without interest—in a bond upon mortgage to Mr. Roberts for the sum of one thousand pounds currency with interest.

I give and bequeath to my father, if then living, or after him, to Colonel Lewis Bouquet, and to his heirs all the effects of any nature, whatsoever, which I may be possessed of in the continent of Europe, without exception. I constitute and appoint my friend, Colonel Frederick Haldimand, my heir and executor, and to him I give and bequeath all and everything which I may die possessed of in North America, without any exception whatever, upon the condition of paying my just debts and above legacies. My estate, consisting for the present in the farm called Long Meadows enlarged, situate in Frederick County, in the Province of Maryland. (Bouquet received the grant for this estate Sept. 16, 1763. It contained, as owned by him, 4,163 acres of very valuable land. Frederick county, Maryland, at that time included Washington county, within whose present limits the estate was located near the Pennsylvania line.) The deeds whereof are now in the possession of the above named,—Roberts.

The said farm to be sold with the saw-mill, tan yard, houses, tenement and appurtenances on the same for the payment of my debts and legacies in the eighteen hundred acres of land above mentioned, to be surveyed for me in this Province and remaining after deducting the five tracts given to Mr. Willing—in my share of the Shepody lands if then in my possession in my apparel, baggage, furniture, stores, &c., in my pay and arrears which may be due me at my death—in my share of the Carolina Plantation after the accounts are fully settled between Messrs. Guinand and the others concerned, all of which I bequeath to Colonel Haldimand, and I hereby annul and declare void, and of no effect, any other will which I may at any time have made previous to this day, as this present will and testament contains my last and real intentions and disposition, and is to take place accordingly. In witness whereof,

I have wrote, (written) signed with my own hand and affixed my seal to this last will and testament, in the City of Philadelphia, in Pennsylvania, this twenty-fifth day of June, in the year of our Lord one thousand seven hundred and sixty five.

Henry Bouquet.

Signed, sealed, published and declared by the testator as his last will and testament in our presence who subscribed the same as witnesses in his presence and at his request.

Benjamin Chew,<br>Jo. Turner,<br>Thos. Turner.

The will was probated Nov. 1, 1765, on oath of the Turners, the other witness, Mr. Chew, being the register general. Soon after this and evidently with a good deal of reluctance, General Bouquet set out for his new station at Pensacola, where he arrived Aug. 23, 1765, in the deadliest season of the year, and at once fell a victim to the fever so fatal to unacclimated persons. The following extract from the *Pennsylvania Magazine* for Thursday October 24, 1765, tells the sad story:

> On Tuesday last arrived the sloop *William*, Captain Rivers, in thirty-six days from Pensacola, by whom we learn ten sail of transports with troops (to relieve those on that station that are going home) arrived there, and that there has been a great mortality among them, ten or twelve dying of a day, amongst which was the gallant and worthy officer, Brigadier General Bouquet. This gentleman had served his Majesty all the last war with great distinction. He was promoted from conscious merit not only unenvied, but even with the approbation and good wishes of all who knew him.
>
> His superior judgement and knowledge of military matters, his experienced a unities, known humanity, remarkable politeness and constant attention to the civil rights of His Majesty's subjects, rendered him an honour to his country and a loss to mankind. He arrived the 23rd of Au-

gust and died September 2. Thus, in the midst of his growing fame and in the full vigour of manhood this superb man, who had faced death unscathed a thousand times in the forests and thickets of Pennsylvania, met his untimely end from insidious disease, just as he was about to begin his career on a new theatre of action in the far distant south.

He died universally regretted, and his character and example were commended by contemporary writers as worthy of imitation by young officers who desired to win a lasting fame in the public service. He sleeps in a soldier's grave, far from home and cindered, far from those who knew him but to love him. But warm and grateful hearts in the North land cherished his memory and fame with fond affection 118 years ago. And although for a time oblivion's waves seemed to have almost engulfed him, yet we see the dawn of a brighter day and feel assured that the fame of Bouquet will shine forth bright and beautiful as in days of yore. In the forum of all grateful hearts, among the descendants of Colonial ancestors or pioneer settlers, a monument deserves to be erected to the memory of Henry Bouquet more enduring than Parian marble or Corinthian brass. Reverently and gratefully I pay him this tribute and would that it were indeed an amaranthine chaplet to adorn and perpetuate his memory, yea to call forth the homage of the good, the brave and the true, as the centuries go marching down the corridors of time.

# Bouquet's Grave Unknown

Bouquet's grave at Pensacola is unmarked and unknown. During the past ten months very thorough researches have been made by the military authorities on the Gulf, but all in vain, as the subjoined letters indicate.

> War Department, Adjutant General's Office,
> Washington, February 13, 1883.

My Dear Sir: Your letter of the 9th inst. enclosing one addressed to our Minister at Great Britain, has been received. It affords me great pleasure to aid you all I can in this matter, and I have accordingly submitted your letter to Mr. Lowell, to the Hon. the Secretary of War, for transmission to the Secretary of State for such action as may be consistent with public interests.

Referring to your inquiry of the 9th *ult.*, respecting the remains of Bouquet, I regret to inform you, that the commanding officer at Fort Barrancas, Fla., to whom your request was referred, reports under the date of the 7th instant, that he has made search and inquiry in Pensacola regarding the whereabouts of General Bouquet's remains, but has not been able to learn anything about them. He further states that the oldest cemetery at Pensacola was commenced in 1780, and that those best posted in the matter have informed him that all the cemeteries at that place were destroyed prior to 1780, and that there is no trace of them left.

The old cemeteries at Pensacola were probably destroyed

in 1781, when that town was besieged and taken by the Spanish General Galvez.

I will make further inquiries regarding Bouquet's remains and apprise you of the result.

    Yours very truly,

R. C. Drum,<br>Adjutant General.

Rev. Cyrus Cort,
Greencastle, Franklin County, Pa.

★★★★★★

War Department, Adjutant Generals Office,<br>Washington, *March 21*, 1883.

Dear Sir: I have received General Hancock's answer to my inquiries regarding Bouquet's remains.

He informs me that upon the receipt of my letter he referred it to several officers who have been stationed at Fort Barrancas, Fla., for any information or suggestions they might have in this matter; that they named certain persons who, they thought, could probably furnish the desired information, but that all efforts in that direction have thus far proved to be unsuccessful.

The commanding officer of Fort Barrancas again visited Pensacola, with a view of obtaining some information of the remains of Bouquet, supposed to have be buried there. He interviewed a. number of gentlemen, old residents of that town, and states that none of them have ever heard of Bouquet.

He also searched the old cemetery, which was deeded by the Spanish to the Catholic church in 1781, but without success, and finally states that—unfortunately—the records of the cemetery as well as those of the Catholic church, were destroyed by fire last summer, and regrets to state that it is impossible to gain any information at Pensacola regarding the whereabouts of Bouquet's remains.

    I am, yours very truly,

R. C. Drum,<br>Adjutant General.

The Rev. Cyrus Cort,
Greencastle, Franklin County, Pa.

General Drum has shown great zeal and persistency in this research. He has always manifested deep interest in the character and career of Colonel Bouquet, and as a Westmorelander of old and honoured lineage, he is anxious to have justice done to the hero of Bushy Run. It remains for the present generation to mark aright the field of Bouquet's greatest triumph by a monument as lasting as the hills which were consecrated by the blood and valour of his heroic soldiers. *Apropos* to this part of my subject I will append a poem, which was written in a freighter on the Iowa prairies, whilst the writer was transporting his horse and household goods from one field of pastoral labour to another, Nov. 19, 1880, the thermometer being several degrees below zero.

# Bouquet's Grave

*He sleeps in an unknown grave,
In a faraway land,
By the South Sea strand,
Bouquet sleeps the sleep of the brave.*

*Sleep on, Oh son of the free!
Where the blood of the Scot,
From the field where you fought,
Ran down to the boundless sea.*

*Ah! was it not grandly meet,
That the gallant Bouquet,
In that land far away,
Should lie where the surges beat.*

*Oh Sea! be an urn for the men,
And a requiem bell
For the hero who fell,
Till the muse shall be grateful again.*

*Alas! 'Tis a burning shame,
That the Keystone state
Should be tardy or late
To cherish the Switzer's fame.*

*Redeemed were your woody hills
By the Swiss and the Scot,
Let them ne'er be forgot
While valour the bosom thrills.*

*Awake! Ye sons of the North!
And the deeds of these men*

*Clasp to your hearts again,*
*And fondly cherish their worth.*

*Oh, land of the brave and free!*
*Bright as the noonday sun,*
*Long as your streams shall run*
*Let the fame of the Switzer be.*

# A Monument Due Bouquet

In an article written for Frank Cowan's paper, on the Bushy Run battle, nearly eleven years ago, I asked the question "does not Westmoreland County, yea all Western Pennsylvania owe a monument to Henry Bouquet?" In my centennial speech at Hannastown, a year ago, I enlarged upon the same thought and, I trust, that in the Providence of God, I may see the day when the dear old county of my nativity will thus honour herself, as well as the grand hero who has made her soil historic ground. All public-spirited people should aid in such a work. It will stimulate the young to emulate one who, amid perils and privations, by sterling merit and conscientious fidelity to duty, rose from obscurity to become the peer of the greatest and best.

It will help to demonstrate that no night of years or changes of human governments and institutions, can obliterate the memory of genuine worth and true manhood, as illustrated in the history of Henry Bouquet.

With Pericles, as amplified by Edward Everett at Gettysburg, we may say of illustrious men "The whole earth is their sepulchre and all time the millennium of their glory." Wherever heroic deeds have been done, wherever the battles of human civilization have been fought and won, that is hallowed ground, full of deepest interest to every thoughtful, true-hearted man.

*These are the shrines to code nor creed confined*
*The Delphian vales, the Palestine, the Meccas of the mind.*

Bushy Run battlefield ought to be, and I feel assured will be looked upon, in years to come, as such a shrine. Here savage barbarism, as represented by Pontiac and Guyasutha, two of its noblest representatives, met the vanguard of civilization, culture and progress, under the matchless leadership of Bouquet. Here, too, was fought and won the battle which virtually established the supremacy of the Anglo-Saxon race, in the great valley of the Mississippi.

*The land is holy where they fought*
*And holy where they fell.*

Not by British blood and valour *per se,* but by Swiss and Scot, Royal Americans, Provincials and Highlanders from Caledonia hills, by these other branches of the great Teutonic host, the Aryan or Indo-Germanic family of nations, was this typical battle fought and won 120 years ago.

It is meet that the German-Swiss and Scotch-Irish elements should possess this goodly land, as they do this day, forming the bone and sinew of Westmoreland's sterling population.

And it is meet that they should not forget the pit out of which they have been dug, nor the rock from which they have been hewn.

The toils and privations of our colonial ancestors should be held in grateful and everlasting remembrance. They braved the perils of old ocean and of life in the Western wilderness, amid savage beasts and more savage men, for the sake of religious principle, and that their children might be freeholders and freemen in the best sense of the term. Let us prize the precious birth-right as something more precious than silver or gold.

Man shall not live by bread alone, but by every word that proceedeth out of the mouth of God.

Ideas, principles, sentiments cultivating a pure and progressive Christian manhood, are of vastly more account than the filthy lucre, on which so many set their hearts.

The scenery and associations of childhood and youth are educational. They stamp their impress upon the soul for weal or for woe. Inspiring historical treasures are beyond all price. Many are the lines of thought and currents of history that centre in and around the honourable and eventful career of Henry Bouquet. As good men did in days of old, so now would I commend his as a character and example worthy of study and imitation by the young and all entrusted with official positions.

# Concluding Remarks

Bouquet willed a large tract of land in Trough Valley, (Huntingdon or Mifflin Co., Pa.,) to Mr. Thos. Willing. This was a brother of Miss Annie Willing, his fair correspondent. His extensive Long Meadows estate in Maryland lay a few miles north or north-east of Hagerstown, Md., and is now owned by the Lehmans, Willems, Cresslers, and others.

Colonel Haldimand, his legatee, and executor, was his special Swiss compatriot and military comrade. He figured somewhat in the Revolutionary War, and became governor-general of Canada, from which post he retired in 1785, to die in his native Switzerland. Many of Bouquet's most valuable papers are included among those of Haldimand, at present, in the British Museum. The time to write a complete biography of the man has not yet arrived.

Mr. G D. Scull, of Philadelphia, residing at Oxford, England, expects to publish a very limited edition of some of these papers during the ensuing year. He claims that on one occasion Bouquet saved Philadelphia from sack and pillage, the proof of which will doubtless appear in his book. I had hoped to be able to refer to this proposed publication in the preparation of this sketch but have been disappointed.

# Pontiac's Submission

Pontiac, for a season remained defiant, even after his confederates had submitted to the terms of Bouquet. When Captain Morris went to him with proposals of peace, he met him on the outskirts of his camp, and refused to take his hand. With flashing eye, he exclaimed, "The English are liars. And yet he spared the captain's life, as he afterwards did that of Lieutenant Fraser, Mr. Croghan, and other peace envoys, although his warriors were anxious to slay them. He sought the country of the Illinois, with 400 warriors, where the flag of France still floated, as it had done since the days of La Salle, Tonti, &c, in 1680.

He urged the different tribes to rise again and fight for the preservation of their race and threatened to destroy those who shirked. French traders had all along led him to expect aid from their great King. At length, he was fully convinced, by replies of French officers, in response to his embassies sent to Fort Chartres and New Orleans, that all hope of help from that quarter was vain. He then gave up the contest and agreed to meet with other confederates at the great council, held by Sir Wm. Johnson, to arrange definitely the terms of peace, secured by the campaigns of Bouquet.

Croghan, who met him repeatedly and experienced this magnanimity in restraining warriors who were anxious to kill the British, peace-agent, speaks thus of the great Ottawa chieftain:

> Pontiac is a shrewd, sensible Indian, of few words, and commands more respect among his own nation than any Indian I ever saw could do among his own tribe.

Late in the fall of 1765 Captain Sterling descended the Ohio in boats and passed up the Mississippi with one hundred Highlanders of the 42nd Regiment to Fort Chartres, of which he took formal possession in the name of Great Britain.

It was fitting that "those veterans whose battle cry," as Parkman says, "had echoed over the bloodiest fields of America," should consummate on the banks of the Father of Waters the work begun at Bushy Run and establish forever Anglo-Saxon supremacy in the new world. In due time Pontiac appeared at the great council held by Sir Wm. Johnson during the latter part of July, 1700. The following are the opening sentences of his speech:

> Father, we thank the Great Spirit for giving us so fine a day to meet upon such great affairs. I speak in the name of all the nations to the westward, of whom I am the master. It is the will of the Great Spirit that we should meet here today; and before him I now take you by the hand. I call him to witness that I speak from the heart; for since I took Colonel Croghan by the hand last year, I have never let go my hold, for I see that the Great Spirit will have us friends.

# Pontiac's Assassination and its Expiation

Everything was amicably adjusted at the council, and Pontiac, with many presents, returned to the Maumee, where he spent one season. He afterwards seems to have located in the region of the Illinois Indians, who were jealous of his presence, and who approved of his assassination. Accounts differ in regard to this affair, Mr. Parkman adopts the Cahokia theory *i.e.*, that Pontiac was killed at that place by an Illinois Indian who had been bribed to do the foul deed by Williamson, an English trader, who feared that Pontiac, while on a drunken spree, was about to stir up trouble against the English, and thus interfere with his traffic. Mr. Matson contends that Pontiac was fatally stabbed by Kineboo, the chief of the Illinois Indians at a council, held near Joliet, in that state.

One thing is certain, the Illinois Indians were held responsible for his assassination. All the tribes that in former days had felt the magic spell of his eloquence and had responded to his bugle can, now leagued together to avenge the death of Pontiac by a war of extermination against the Illinois Indians.

The following extract I take from an article which I prepared for the *Guardian* for August, 1882, on the basis of Matson's theory:

> Runners were sent to the Winnebagos, of the North, and the Kickapoos, of the South-west, who agreed, to help avenge the death of the great Pontiac. Over the remains a council was held by the allies, who swore by the great

Manito of war not to lay down the tomahawk until the fallen chieftain's death should be avenged by the destruction of the Illinois Indians, who abetted the cowardly deed of Kineboo. The Miamis united with the tribes already mentioned, and Bernet, the white outlaw, also with a band of warriors, joined in the bloody strife.

The combined forces made the most formidable Indian army ever collected in the West. Death and annihilation to the Illinois was the savage oath of the ferocious avengers. The smaller towns along the Illinois River were first destroyed, and finally La Vantum, their great capital, which was defended by their bravest warriors, was suddenly assaulted. The skull and cross bones of Pontiac were borne on a red pole by the avengers. Their first attack met with a bloody repulse. A council of war was called by the invaders, at which the leading war chiefs, with fiery eloquence, advocated that nothing short of extermination of the Illinoisans would meet the demands of the case or be acceptable to the great Manito of war.

The Illinois warriors had spent much of the night in dancing and premature rejoicing over the repulse of the assailants and were taken by surprise in the morning. After terrific carnage, the allies were again repulsed with great slaughter. But again, and again they returned with reinforcements to the conflict. Thus, for twelve long hours the carnival of death went on in and around La Vantum, the great Indian city of the West. Night came on, and still the battle raged, until a heavy ram storm put an end to hostilities. During the darkness and storm the Illinois Indians crossed the Illinois river in their canoes and ascended Starved Rock, the old site of Fort St. Louis, where Tonti had so signally repulsed the Iroquois.

Here the remnant of 1200 Illinois Indians, including 300 warriors, rallied and thought themselves secure. But the allied forces, not content with the destruction of the town and other property of the Illinois, quickly surrounded the Rock, determined to avenge the death of Pontiac by the complete annihilation of all who in anyway approved of his assassination. With ferocious yells they rushed up the rugged pathway on the only accessible side of the rocky summit. But brave and desperate Illinois warriors, with war clubs and tomahawks, sent them bleeding and mangled down the steep declivity.

Again, and again did the fierce avengers attempt to storm the almost impregnable heights. Many were slain as soon as they reached the summit and hurled over the precipice into the river below. After losing many of their bravest warriors, the allies gave up the assault and began the slow and tedious work of starving out the besieged Illinoisans. At the time of the attack upon the town a French and Indian half-breed warrior, named Belix, who had greatly distinguished himself in previous battles, was being married to the beautiful daughter of Chief Kineboo. When the assault was made upon the Rock, Belix stood foremost and most valiant among the defenders and with his war-club dealt deathblows upon many of the assailants. His bride stood nearby to encourage her gallant lord but when she saw him fall with skull cloven by a tomahawk, she uttered a wild scream and sprang over the Rock, falling from crag to crag until her lifeless body dropped into the river below.

Fifty-one years had elapsed since the rock had been abandoned by the French, and the palisades and earth-works afforded but little protection against sharp-shooters who took possession of neighbouring cliffs and joined in a galling fire upon the Illinois. Kineboo, whose rash and dastardly act had precipitated the war, was killed in this way. But soon a rampart, sufficient to ward off bullets was erected by the besieged along the exposed edges of the precipices. But the worst enemy now began to assail them. Hunger began to gnaw at their vitals with remorseless tooth. The small supply of provisions, brought along in their flight from La Vantum, were soon exhausted. The Rock of refuge became an altar of sacrifice, of whole burnt offering, to the Illinois in the end; for their relentless foes never relaxed in the siege until the last Illinois but one had perished.

A warrior, the solitary exception let himself down by a buckskin cord into the river on a dark and stormy night and escaped, but all the rest, warriors, squaws and papooses perished. Some of the squaws, in the delirium of hunger and thirst, would spring with their infants into the river. Warriors would make a sortie only to be slam or driven back by the merciless avengers. Some feasted on the dead. The death-song was chanted, and at last, when a final assault was made, only a few feeble survivors remained to be tomahawked. Thus, perished the once powerful and arrogant Illinois, and thus terribly was the assassination of the great Pontiac avenged.

Great must have been the magnetism of the man in life and death who marshalled the conspiracy which nearly drove the English east of the Alleghenies, and which combined the savage hosts of the lakes and the prairies to expiate the deep damnation of his taking off by a holocaust that is unparalleled even in the history of savage warfare and retaliation. Well may the old site of Fort St. Louis, on the Illinois River, near Ottawa, Illinois, the scene of the first white settlement in the Mississippi valley, two hundred years ago, be called Starved Rock, in commemoration of that closing tragedy and catastrophe in the history of the great tribe whose name is perpetuated not only by the river along which they roved, fished and hunted, and fought their numerous foes, but also by the title of one of the greatest and most prosperous states in the American Union.

Thus, was expiated the death of Pontiac, over whose grave, as Parkman says:

More blood was poured out in atonement than flowed from the veins of the slaughtered heroes on the corpse of Patroclus.

Let justice be done to the memory of the man who broke the eastern wing of the great conspiracy at Bushy Run, Aug. 6, 1763, and rolled back the advancing tide of savage barbarism. All honour to Colonel Henry Bouquet and his heroic army of deliverance, who consecrated by their blood and valour, the green hills of old Westmoreland and made them historic forever.

# Westmoreland County Before and During the Revolution

Westmoreland County was created by Pennsylvania provincial authorities in 1773, and originally included all that part of the State west of Laurel Hill. A dozen other counties have since been created out of the same territory, so that for Western Pennsylvania it may be said that "Old Westmoreland" was the mother of counties.

Hannastown, a hamlet a few miles north-east of Greensburg, was the first county seat. Here justice was first dispensed, west of the Alleghenies, according to the civil code. William Crawford, afterwards burnt by the Indians, was the first presiding justice, and Arthur St. Clair was the first prothonotary. The first court fixed the price of a gill of whiskey at four pence; toddy, one smiling; West India rum, six pence; cider, per quart, one shilling six pence; strong beer, per quart, sixpence.

The jail was made of rough, unhewn logs. Punishments were fines, whipping, standing in pillory or stocks, cropping on ears and branding.

Rape, sodomy, robbery, mayhem, arson, burglary, witchcraft and concealing of a bastard child were punishable with death, as well as murder. Virginia set up rival claims to a large part of the territory included in Westmoreland county, and created West Augusta county to cover it. Lord Dunmore, her Tory Governor, organised a court at Pittsburgh Feb. 21, 1775, to offset the claims of Pennsylvania. Dr. John Connolly, a resident of Pittsburgh, was the Virginia agent, and representative of Dunmore. He published a manifesto Jan. 1, 1774, inviting settlers to meet at Pittsburgh on the 25th *proximo* for conference, assuring them of the protection of Virginia.

Arthur St. Clair, a justice of the peace of Westmoreland, issued a warrant and had Connolly arrested for a short time and confined in the log jail at Hannastown. Connolly, after his release, issued warrants and arrested the Westmoreland justices of the peace. The conflict continued for about a year. Virginia's claims were recognized at Fort Pitt and in the Monongahela region. Yohogania County was created Nov. 30, 1776, out of part of Augusta and included the greater part of Alleghany and Washington counties. Virginia courts were held for five years under these auspices. Virginia's price for lands being cheaper than those of Pennsylvania, the settlers in those regions generally sided with her in the dispute. At Bushy Run, Hannastown and Ligonier, with adjacent settlements, Pennsylvania interests and claims were upheld. This conflict of jurisdiction caused great trouble and uneasiness, which was not allayed fully until the completion of the western end of Mason and Dixon's line, after the Revolution.

From the date of Bouquet's peace, dictated to the Indians on the Muskingum, until the outbreak of the Revolution, there was comparative peace and tranquillity, so far as the Indians were concerned. The fur traders plied their lucrative traffic without molestation. The country began to fill up rapidly.

When the War of Independence began, the sectional disputes were forgotten and a common purpose was manifested to resist the encroachments of Great Britain. Hannastown has the honour of not only being the first seat of civil justice, west of the Alleghanies, but of leading the van in sounding the note of defiance in a formal public declaration of the sentiments that stirred the heart of the persecuted colonies. On the sixteenth of May, 1775, a convention was held at Hannastown, which denounced the acts of British usurpation and tyranny, and took measures to provide for the common defence.

Westmoreland was prompt in electing delegates, July 8, 1776, to attend the convention, which met in Philadelphia, July 15,

1776, to lay the foundations of a government, based on the authority of the people only.

That convention included many of the best men of the state—wise in counsel, brave and energetic in action. Men like Franklin, Clymer, Hiester, and Rittenhouse. Westmoreland sent as her delegates—James Barr, Edward Cook, James Smith, John Moore, John Carmichael, James Perry, John McClellan and Christian Lavingair.

Before taking their seats or casting their votes, they were required to subscribe to the following:

> I — —do profess faith in God, the Father, and in Jesus Christ, His Eternal Son, the true God, and in the Holy Spirit, one God blessed forever more; and do acknowledge the Holy Scripture of the Old and New Testament to be given by divine inspiration.

A very correct and orthodox profession of the fundamental doctrines of Christianity. The convention adjourned September 28, 1776, after framing an excellent form of government, by the people and for the people. In fact, their work has formed the basis for all the state constitutions since adopted. And now came the horrors of war. To the everlasting disgrace and infamy of Great Britain, it must be said that she offered large bounties to cruel savages for the scalps of the frontier settlers, men, women and children.

The British Governor, Hamilton, who had control at Detroit and along the northern frontiers, gave standing rewards for scalps, but offered none for prisoners. In consequence the Indians compelled the poor captives to carry their plunder to the immediate vicinity of Detroit, where, after having endured indescribable sufferings during the journey through the wilderness, the poor creatures were put to death and scalped in cold blood to get the bounty. De Peyster, under orders from Haldimand, acted more humanely as commandant at Detroit. He encouraged the Indians to bring in live meat, as the prisoners from the borders were called, rather than scalps, which he did not like to see.

In this way he saved 300 frontier prisoners from a barbarous death. Prowling bands of savages continually ravaged the borders, and Westmoreland was a favourite resort for the scalping parties. The old war path of the Catawbas and Cherokees from the south and south-west, with a tributary trail or path from Tennessee and Kentucky, went right through the heart of Westmoreland to the headwaters of the Susquehanna, in western New York, where lived the Iroquois, or Six Nations, their inveterate enemies. After the conquest of the southern tribes by their powerful northern foes, they made periodical trips to pay tribute or show proper obeisance to the conquerors.

The Mohawk Pluggy, located on the eastern branch of the Scioto, with a lawless and miscellaneous gang of marauders, made frequent forays into the settlements along the Ohio and its branches.

Generals Hand and McIntosh, Colonel Brodhead and General Irvine commanded Fort Pitt during the Revolution, and although many expeditions were projected and a few abortive ones undertaken to carry the war into the Indian country, nothing serious was ever accomplished in that line to check the repeated incursions of the savages. Such a campaign and commander as carried terror to their hearts in their own native haunts in 1764, would have secured safety and tranquillity to a large extent. But the desultory and fragmentary efforts put forth from time to time for aggressive movements against the savages and as a rule only resulted in greater hardships for the frontier settlers.

McKee, the Girty's and other tories who had grudge against the frontier settlers, led on the savage demons with great craft and daring against the exposed frontiers. In April, 1778, a Westmorelander wrote:

> God only knows what may be the fate of this county; but at present it wears a dismal aspect.

May 1, 1779, another wrote,

> The savages are continually making depredations among us; not less than forty people have been killed, wounded

or captured this spring.

A year later and the prospect was still more gloomy. Over forty settlers had been slain in the Monongahela region, and the raids were frequent from the northern Allegheny regions.

Butterfield wrote:

> It really began to look as though Westmoreland would again become a wilderness.

The people, in a half starving condition, huddled in and about the forts and block-houses. The troops at Fort Pitt were ragged, unpaid, poorly fed, and of course discontented and inefficient. In August the Maryland corps deserted their posts on the frontier of Westmoreland, and in a body marched across the mountains. Lochry and his 150 picked men were surprised and destroyed in 1781. Crawford, another county official, met with terrible disaster and death in 1782; and thus, the chapter of horrors and frontier suffering goes on. Brodhead and some of his subordinate officers got at loggerheads, and in the midst of quarrels among officers at Fort Pitt the work of desolation prospered.

General Irvine was appointed, but although many campaigns were talked about, none but such as Crawford's, Williamson's, &c, badly managed affairs, were actualized. The main army was engaged in the last death grapples with the British Lion along the Atlantic coast, and the western settlers were largely left to the mercy of the savages.

The British were emboldened even to fit out an expedition to capture Fort Pitt. Three hundred British and Tories, and five hundred Indians, assembled with twelve pieces of artillery, on Lake Jadagua (Chatauqua), in 1782, with this intention. Having learned, through a spy, that the fort was much stronger than had been supposed, the main object of the expedition was given up. The usual method of border warfare was then adopted, and marauding bands went into the different settlements. A feeling of unrest and apprehension pervaded the frontier. Many had been shot down and scalped, and prisoners carried off from the immediate vicinity of Forts Walthour, Klingensmith, &c. This sense of alarm found very timely and forcible representation in the petition of German settlers on Brush Creek, addressed to General Irvine, commander at Fort Pitt, June 22, 1782.

It sets forth the despondency and distress of the people on account of continued calamities (Crawford's fate had just been learned). They speak of the great peril attending the gathering of the harvest, nearly ripe, and beg for some troops to protect them as they seek to gather in the crops which are needed to save them from famine—as much to be dreaded as the scalping knife. This petition was signed by ancestors of many living Westmorelanders, *viz*.: George, Christopher, Joseph and Michael Waldhauer, (Walthour.) Abraham and Joseph Studabedker, Michael and Jacob Byerly, John and Jacob Ruthdorf, Frederick Williard, —— Wiesskoph (Whitehead), Abram Schneider, Peter and Jacob Loutzenheiser, Hanover Davis, Conrad Zulten, Garret Pendegrast and John Kammerer This petition is given by Butterfield, without the names of signers, on pages 300-301 of his valuable book, *Washington Irvine Correspondence*.

# Attack on Hannastown

Three weeks later, July 13, 1782, a large detachment of the aforesaid Chatauqua expedition burst upon Hannastown, the county seat of Westmoreland. They burned the town, and came very near capturing the fort, into which a few of the frightened settlers, with Michael Huffnagle, the prothonotary at their head, had fled for safety. Captain Matthew Jack, by his courage and presence mind, saved many lives on that disastrous day, as he rode gallantly from point to point, even through the encompassing lines of whooping savages.

Miller's station, nearby, was raided by the Indians, and the greater part of a wedding party was captured, including the wife and daughters, of Robert Hanna. Captain Brownlee, and several others, were tomahawked, after being led captives a few miles. Dwellings were destroyed, together with many horses and cattle. The settlers were so terror-stricken that the ripened harvest was not gathered in many places, and great want ensued. Connolly, the renegade Tory, General St. Clair had confined in the log jail at Hannastown, is supposed to have led this party, together with Guyasutha, the famous Seneca chief.

About twenty persons were killed or captured in this foray. On the 13th of July, 1882, the centennial of this attack and repulse of the Indians and Tories at Hannastown, was celebrated by a large assemblage of Westmorelanders, in the woods near the old site of Hannastown. Hon. Jacob Turney presided, and made the opening address. Addresses were also made by Hon. Daniel Kane, Judge Bigham, Ex-Senator Cowan, and Rev. Cyrus Cort.

# Religious Characteristics of Early Settlers

It is gratifying to know that amid their dangers and hardships, those Teutonic pioneers in old Westmoreland forgot not the God of their fathers.

On May 1, 1782, when the Reformed Cœtus (Synod) met at Reading, Pa., a petition was received from "A congregation in Westmoreland County, near Pittsburg, in the back part of Pennsylvania, a new settlement, where no ministers have yet been." They "very earnestly entreated for a good minister, to whom they promise to pay annually eighty pounds sterling, besides other necessaries of life."

Rev. John William Weber, having expressed a willingness to go west and take charge of this mission enterprise, the Reverend Cœtus recommended him and advised the Westmoreland people to give him a regular call. He arrived in Sept., 1782, and preached through what now constitutes Westmoreland, Washington and Fayette counties, and at Fort Pitt, where the traveller Schopf met him in October, 1782. The congregations at Harolds and Brush Creek were organised a few months after Rev. Weber's arrival in Westmoreland. Here worshipped the Turneys, Drums, Barnharts, Marchands, Trubys, Mechlings, Kemmerers, Kifers, Klines, Byerlys, Whiteheads, Saams, Klingensmiths, Kunkles, Walthours, Baughmans, Thomases, Detars, Harolds, Grosses, Henrys, Corts, Keppels, Kiehls, Shrums, Painters, and many other ancestors of Reformed and Lutheran families.

Previous to the coming of Rev. Weber many of these German pioneers used to meet at the house of Loutzenheiser and Davis to read the scriptures, sing the sweet hymns of the German fatherland, hear a sermon read by some competent person, and engage in other religious services as best they could.

They frequently carried their rifles with them, when they went to worship in the early days of Rev. Weber's ministry. Prowling savages lurked in the thickets for many years. Amid such perils and privations, those pioneer settlers carved out homes for their children and turned the western wilderness of Penn's woods into a fruitful field. Surely a grateful posterity should honour their memory and rise up and call them blessed, while enjoying the goodly fruits of their pioneer toil.

At a still earlier date the Scotch-Irish, led by pastors Finley, Power, McMillan, Dodd, Smith, &c, occupied the Sewickly and other settlements, and already in 1781, the old Redstone Presbytery was organised. "The incursions of savages" prevented the first meeting being held at Laurel Hill, the appointed place, and so it met at Pigeon Creek.

It is meet, as already said, that the descendants of the hardy Scotch-Irish and German-Swiss should occupy the green hills and fertile valleys of old Westmoreland. By the blood and the sweat and the toil of their pioneer ancestors, this goodly land has been rescued from savage barbarism. Hallowed be the memory of the brave men and women who nobly stood in the breach in the hour of trial and danger.

Pennsylvania has been compared to a sleeping giant, not yet fully conscious of her vast power and resources. With unappreciated modesty, she has failed to assert her rights, and especially has she neglected to cherish aright the rich legacies of the past, bequeathed by an honest and patriotic ancestry. It behoves us to gather up the historic treasures that rightfully belong to our grand old Keystone commonwealth.

Our own self-respect and independent manhood demands this. It is no less a duty to posterity than a debt of gratitude to our heroic ancestry. The educational effect will be stimulating and ennobling in all respects. For the sake of religious principle, our forefathers crossed old ocean's wave and braved the dangers of pioneer life in the new world. In the midst of untold penis, they were true to the principles of civil and religious liberty, as we have already seen, and here on our native hills was fought the decisive battle of Christian civilization against heathen barbarism.

# Addenda

Referring back under "Forbes expedition and dispute with Washington," it is proper to remark that Bouquet and Washington were personally on good terms and did not impugn each other's motives.

Many persons will doubtless feel prompted to contribute toward the erection of a monument to Henry Bouquet, after reading the record of his gallant achievements. All such will please send funds or written pledges to James Gregg, Chairman of Finance Committee, Greensburg, Pa., subject to the disposal of the Executive Committee—Coulter, Kline and Gregg—for that purpose.

P. S.—After this pamphlet was nearly all in type, I learned that at a meeting held subsequent to June 19, 1883, it was decided to invite the following gentlemen to address the meeting at Bushy Run battlefield, Aug. 6, 1883, *viz*:

Hon. James G. Blaine, of Washington, D. C.; Dr. Samuel Wilson, of Allegheny City, Pa.; General James A. Beaver, of Bellefonte, Pa.; Hon. William S. Stenger, of Harrisburg, Pa.; Rev. Cyrus Cort, of Greencastle. Pa.; Wm. M. Darlington, of Pittsburgh, Pa.; Hon. W. U. Hensel, of Lancaster, Pa.; Hon. Silas M. Clark, of Indiana, Pa.; Hon. Wm. Koontz, of Somerset, Pa.

Poem.—Frank Cowan, Esq., of Greensburg, Pa.

# The History of Bouquet's Expeditions

# Contents

| | |
|---|---|
| Publishers' Notice | 149 |
| Francis Parkman's Preface | 151 |
| Biographical Sketch of Henry Bouquet | 155 |
| Introduction | 159 |
| Colonel Bouquet's Expedition Against the Ohio Indians in the Year 1764 | 177 |
| Postscript | 211 |
| Reflections on the War with the Savages of North America | 214 |
| The Temper and Genius of the Indians | 215 |
| General Idea of an Establishment of Light Troops for the Service of the Woods | 224 |
| Appendix 1 | 239 |
| Appendix 2 | 242 |
| Appendix 3 | 246 |
| Appendix 4 | 247 |
| Appendix 5 | 250 |

# Publishers' Notice

On offering to our patrons the *Account of General Bouquet's Expedition against the Ohio Indians in* 1764, as the first of the reprints of the *Ohio Valley Historical Series,* we may premise that we have been urged thereto by the rarity of the volume and its intrinsic value as an authentic and reliable narrative of one of the earliest British military expeditions into the territory northwest of the Ohio River.

This work was published at Philadelphia in 1765, reprinted at London the following year; and an edition in French, by C. G. F. Dumas, was issued at Amsterdam in 1769.

Mr. Francis Parkman has kindly furnished us with a few prefatory words. The proper introduction, however, to this work, and indeed to all the fragmentary accounts of the later struggles of the white and Indian races in the Central West, is his *History of the Conspiracy of Pontiac*, of which this expedition was one of the results. We cannot too earnestly recommend its perusal to our readers. His wonderfully clear and exact knowledge of Indian character, and its faithful portrayal in his introductory chapters, together with his minute accounts of their tribal divisions, their internal differences, their modes of warfare, the nature of their governments, and his general review of the "situation," cannot fail to be of great service in attaining an intelligent understanding of the story of the Indian wars in the West, and the trials and hardships of the sturdy pioneers, whose bloody struggles and anxious labours laid the foundation of the present prosperity of this region.

Mr. Parkman has also translated for us M. Dumas' biographical sketch of General Bouquet prefixed to the French edition. We regret that we are, at present, unable to give a more detailed history of his transactions in this country, the most active and interesting period of his life, concerning which M. Dumas' sketch is very meagre, passing over in silence his important services as one of the commanders of the Royal American Corps, his connection with the former expedition against Fort Duquesne, in 1758, under General Forbes, and his celebrated controversy with General—then Colonel—Washington as to the route which that expedition should take from Carlisle to Fort Duquesne. (For particulars of this controversy, see Craig's *Olden Time*, Vol. 1, published at Pittsburgh, in 1846, and Sparks *Life and Writings of Washington*, Vol. 2.) The one urgently advocated by General Bouquet, through Raystown, now Bedford, and Loyal Hanna, was adopted, and the marked advantage of this road in subsequent military operations, and. in encouraging the settlement of Western Pennsylvania, evinced his practical wisdom and forethought.

We would call the attention of our readers to the successful manner in which, by the "Osborne Process," the American Photo-Lithographic Company have reproduced the map, plans, and the two plates by Benjamin West, in facsimile of the originals.

A former edition for the Ohio Valley Series was published in 1867, in which the old-style spelling and form of type of the original edition was used, but in this reprinting, it has been thought best to modernize the style, and make it plainer and better for current reading.

# Francis Parkman's Preface

The peace of 1763 was the beginning of a new epoch in the history of this continent. The vast region from the Alleghanies to the Rocky Mountains had been explored, mapped out, and, in good measure, occupied by the French. Their forts, missions, and trading posts—the centres, in some cases, of little colonies—were scattered throughout the Valley of the Mississippi and on the borders of all the Great Lakes. They had gained a controlling influence over the Indians, and by the right of discovery and of colonization they regarded the country as their own. When Wolfe and Amherst conquered Canada, the vast but frail fabric of French empire in the West crumbled to the dust. An industrial democracy, not a military monarchy married to the hierarchy of Rome, was thenceforth to assume the mighty task for conquering this rich wilderness for civilization.

To the Indian tribes, its natural owners, the change was nothing but a disaster. They had held, in a certain sense, the balance of power between the rival colonies of France and England. Both had bid for their friendship, and both competed for the trade with them. The French had been the more successful. Their influence was predominant among all the interior tribes, while many of the border Indians, old allies of the English, had of late abandoned them in favour of their rivals.

While the French had usually gained the good will, often the ardent attachment, of the tribes with whom they came in contact, the English, for the most part, had inspired only jealousy and dislike. This dislike was soon changed to the most intense hatred. Lawless traders and equally lawless speculators preyed on the Indians; swarms of squatters invaded the lands of the border tribes and crowded them from their homes.

No race on earth has a more intense and unyielding individuality than the Indians. To the weakness and vices inseparable from all low degrees of human development, he joins a peculiar reserve and pride. He will not coalesce with superior races and will not imitate them. When enslaved he dies, kills himself, kills his master, or runs away. It has been his lot to be often hated, but seldom thoroughly despised.

His race has never received a nickname, and he has never served as a subject of amusement. There is some humour in him, but he is too grim a figure to be laughed at. One is almost constrained to admire the inflexible obstinacy with which he clings to his own personality, rejects the advances of civilization, and prefers to die as he has lived.

Such, indeed, is the alternative; and it was after the peace of 1763 that this inexorable sentence of civilization or destruction was first proclaimed over the continent in tones no longer doubtful.

That the Indians understood the crisis it would be rash to affirm; but they felt it without fully understanding it. The result was the great Indian war under Pontiac. The tribes leagued together and rose to drive the English into the sea. All the small posts of the interior were captured from the English, and the frontiers swept with fire. The two great forts, Detroit and Fort Pitt, alone withstood the assailants, and both were reduced to extremity. Pontiac himself, with the tribes of the Lakes, beleaguered Detroit, while the Delawares and Shawanees, with some of the Wyandottes laid siege, in their barbarous way, to Fort Pitt, or Pittsburgh. Other bands of the same tribes meanwhile ravaged the frontiers of Pennsylvania, burning houses, murdering settlers, laying waste whole districts, and producing an indescribable distress and consternation.

This is the point where the ensuing narrative begins. Happily, for the distracted borders and the distressed garrison, a gallant Swiss officer, Henry Bouquet, then commanded at Philadelphia, and he was ordered to march, with what troops he could collect, to the relief of Fort Pitt. A similar attempt had been made, with greater means and with fewer obstacles, to relieve Detroit and the result had been a deplorable defeat; but Bouquet, an experienced officer, a man of science and a man of sense, proved himself in every way equal to the emergency. The story of this almost desperate attempt is given in the introductory part of the following narrative. The events recounted in the body of the book belong to the succeeding year.

The Indians defeated by Bouquet at Bushy Run, and foiled by Gladwyn before Detroit, had lost heart and hope. General Bradstreet led a body of troops up the lakes to force them to a substantial and permanent peace; while Bouquet, with a similar object, marched into the untrodden wilderness of Ohio. Bradstreet's share of the combined expedition was ill-managed, and but partially successful; yet, while failing to do his own part thoroughly, he took it upon himself to accomplish that assigned to his brother commander.

Bouquet rejected his interference, disregarded the unauthorized treaties he had made, and pursued his march with results which the narrative itself will show. I have examined the original documents on which it is based and can testify that they have been faithfully followed.

The authorship of the *Historical Account of the Expedition* against the Ohio Indians, has been ascribed., by Rich, Allibone, and others, to Thomas Hutchins, at that time Geographer of the United States, who supplied the map; but the following extract from a letter of Dr. William Smith, Provost of the College of Philadelphia, dated January 13, 1766, seems a sufficient proof that the credit belongs to him. He writes to Sir William Johnson:

Mr. Croghan set out the day before I expected he would, else I proposed sending you a copy of Bouquet's *Expedition to Muskingum,* which I drew up from some papers he favoured me with, and which is reprinted in England, and has had a very favourable reception.

Mr. A. R. Spofford, the intelligent custodian of the Library of Congress, first made this contemporary evidence known, having discovered the letter in the Force collection of papers, lately acquired by that Library.

Francis Parkman, Boston, August, 1868.

# Biographical Sketch of Henry Bouquet

Henry Bouquet was a man of a fine person, a superior understanding, and a feeling heart. He made no claim to the good opinion of others, neither did he solicit it. All were compelled to esteem him, and hence there were many of his profession who thought they could, dispense with loving him. Firmness, intrepidity, calmness, presence of mind in the greatest dangers, virtues so essential in a commander, were natural to him. His presence inspired confidence and impressed respect, encouraged his friends and confounded his foes.

He was born at Rolle, in the canton of Berne, in Switzerland. (Rolle is a small town in the canton of Vaud. Together with the greater part of the Vaudois territory, it was formerly under the government of Berne, and regarded as a part of that canton. It is on the northern borders of the Lake of Geneva.—F. P.) In 1736, being then seventeen years old, he was received as a cadet in the regiment of Constant, in the service of L. H. P. (*Leurs Hautes Puissances*—i.e., The States General of Holland.—F. P.), and in 1738 he obtained the commission of ensign in the same regiment. Thence he passed into that of into that of Roguin, in the service of the King of Sardinia, and. distinguished, himself first as first lieutenant, and afterward as adjutant, in the memorable and ably-conducted campaigns of the wars which that great prince sustained against the combined forces of France and Spain.

At the Battle of Cony, being ordered to occupy a piece of ground at the brink of a precipice, he led his men thither in such a way that not one of them saw that they were within two steps of destruction should the enemy force the position. Meanwhile, calmly watching the movements of both armies, he made his soldiers observe, in order to distract their attention, that these movements could be seen much better by the light of the moon than in broad daylight.

The accounts, no less exact than interesting, which he sent to Holland of the operations of these campaigns, came to the knowledge of His Serene Highness, the late Prince of Orange, and induced him to engage this officer in the service of the Republic. In consequence, Mr. Bouquet entered as captain commandant, with the rank of lieutenant colonel, into the regiment of Swiss Guards, newly formed at the Hague, in 1748, and was immediately chosen to go, jointly with Generals Burmannia and Cornabe, to receive from the French the places in the Low Countries which they were about to evacuate, and to arrange the return of the prisoners of war which France gave up to the Republic in conformity with the Treaty of Aix-la-Chapelle. A few months after, Lord Middleton invited him to accompany him in his travels in France and Italy.

On his return to The Hague, he devoted every moment which his regimental duties allowed to the careful study of the military art, and above all of mathematics, which are the foundation of it. The intimate relations which he formed with Professors Hemsterhuis, Konig, and Allamand, and with several other learned men in every branch of science, greatly facilitated his acquisition of the thorough knowledge which afterward gave him a yet higher distinction and caused him to appear with such advantage in the vast theatre of the war kindled between France and England in 1754. (Bouquet always retained his fondness for the society of men of science. When in command at Philadelphia, he formed an intimacy with the botanist Bertram.—F. P.)

As this war obliged England to send troops to America, it was proposed to raise a corps, under the name of Royal Americans, formed of three battalions under one commander, the officers of which were to be indifferently either Americans or foreigners, but in all cases men of capacity and experience.

✶✶✶✶✶✶

The "Royal American Regiment" was to consist of four battalions of one thousand men each, the ranks to be filled in great measure from the German and other continental settlers of Pennsylvania and Maryland. Fifty of the officers might be foreign Protestants, but the colonel must be a natural-born subject. See *Act to enable His Majesty to grant commissions to a certain number of foreign Protestants,* 29 George II., c. 5. The first colonel was John, Earl of Loudoun, but Colonels J. Stanwix, Joseph Dussaux, C. Jeffereys, and James Provost, commanded the four battalions respectively. See *Army List.* The Royal American Regiment is now the Sixtieth Rifles.—F. P.

✶✶✶✶✶✶

This plan, favoured by the Duke or Cumberland, was carried into execution, though altered and mutilated by an opposing faction. Mr. Bouquet and his intimate friend, Mr. Haldimand, were the first to whom those charged with it turned their eyes, and they were urged to serve in this brigade as lieutenant colonels. Both had already reached that rank at The Hague, and by a singular freak of fortune, the officer who was to command them in America was their inferior in Europe. This made them hesitate for some time. Nevertheless, at the urgent persuasion of Sir Joseph Yorke, and upon a promise being made them that they should be placed immediately, as colonels-*commandant*, on a footing of equality wren the colonel-in-chief of the brigade, they were induced to accept the commissions offered them. As soon as their resolution was taken, they were charged to attract into the corps a sufficient number of good officers, both for the engineer and the artillery service. There was no reason to regret that this matter was entrusted to them. Most of these officers were drawn from the armies of the Republic, and they have answered the expectations of those who chose them in a manner which has done honour to both.

I have not entered into a detailed account of the plan which called into existence the brigade of which I have just spoken, for this would have led me too far. I shall content myself with saying, that its origin, and the favour with which it was received, were due to pure accident; but that its happy execution is solely to be ascribed to the discernment of Sir Joseph Yorke, and to his zeal for his country. It is chiefly, then, to him, that the British Empire owes the distinguished services which these brave officers have rendered it. (Major General Sib Joseph Yorke was appointed British Plenipotentiary to the States General in 1751. He had been *aide-de-camp* to the Duke of Cumberland at the Battle of Fontenoy. In 1788 he was raised to the peerage as Baron Dover. He died without issue in 1792.—F. P.)

To return to Mr. Bouquet: On his arrival in America, his integrity, as well as his great capacity, soon acquired for him a great credit in the Colonies, especially in Pennsylvania and Virginia respected by the soldiers, in credit with all who had a share in the internal government of these provinces, universally esteemed and loved, he had but to ask, and he obtained all that it was possible to grant, because it was believed that he asked nothing but what was necessary and proper, and that all would be faithfully employed for the services of the king and the provinces. This good understanding between the civil and military authorities contributed. to his success quite as much, as his ability.

Immediately after the conclusion of peace with the Indians, the king made him brigadier general and commandant of his troops in all the Southern Colonies of British America. He died at Pensacola lamented by his friends and universally regretted. (His death must have occurred in the autumn of 1765, not long after his return from this "Expedition against the Ohio Indians," for, in the *Gentleman's Magazine,* London, for January, 1766, we find the following among the promotions in the British Army: "Aug. Provost, Esq., Lieut. Colonel of the 60th Reg., in room of H. Bouquet, dec.") I wish that the Colonies, which I sincerely love, may have a long succession of such defenders. The young officers who read this, will permit me to propose him as a model for their imitation, and an example well fitted to excite in them a noble emulation. It is to his honour that I have undertaken this translation, and it is to his memory that I dedicate it.

# Introduction

The general peace, concluded between Great Britain, France and Spain, in the year 1762, although viewed in different lights by persons variously affected in the mother country, was nevertheless universally considered as a most happy event in America.

To behold the French, who had so long instigated and supported the Indians, in the most destructive wars and cruel depredations on our frontier settlements, at last compelled to cede all Canada, and restricted to the western side of Mississippi, was what we had long wished, but scarcely hoped an accomplishment of in our own days. The precision with which our boundaries were expressed, admitted of no ground for future disputes, and was matter of exultation to everyone who understood and regarded the interest of these colonies. We had now the pleasing prospect of "entire" security from all "molestation of the Indians, since French intrigues could no longer be employed to seduce, or French force to support them." (The several quotations in this introduction are taken from the Annual Register, 1763, which is written with great elegance and truth, so far as the author appears to have been furnished with materials.)

Unhappily, however, we were disappointed in this expectation:

> Our danger arose from that very quarter, in which we imagined ourselves in the most perfect security; and just at the time when we concluded the Indians to be entirely awed, and almost subjected by our power, they suddenly fell upon the frontiers of our most valuable settlements, and upon all our out-lying forts, with

such unanimity in the design, and with such savage fury in the attack, as we had not experienced, even in the hottest times of any former war.

Several reasons have been assigned for this perfidious conduct on their part; such as an omission of the usual presents, and some settlements made on lands not yet purchased from them. But these causes, if true, could only affect a few tribes, and never could have formed so general a combination against us. The true reason seems to have been a jealousy of our growing power, heightened by their seeing the French almost wholly driven out of America, and a number of forts now possessed by us, which commanded the great lakes and rivers communicating with them, and awed the whole Indian country. They probably imagined that they beheld "in every little garrison the germ of a future colony," and thought it incumbent on them to make one general and timely effort to crush our power in the birth.

By the papers in the Appendix, a general idea may be formed of the strength of the different Indian nations surrounding our settlements, and their situation with respect to each other.

The Shawanese, Delawares and other Ohio tribes, took the lead in this war, and seem to, have begun it rather too precipitately, before the other tribes in confederacy with them, were ready for action.

Their scheme appears to have been projected with much deliberate mischief in the intention, and more than usual skill in the system of execution. They were to make one general and sudden attack upon our frontier settlements in the time of harvest, to destroy our men, corn, cattle, &c. as far as they could penetrate, and to starve our outposts, by cutting off their supplies, and all communication with the inhabitants of the Provinces.

In pursuance of this bold and bloody project, they fell suddenly upon our traders whom they had invited into their country, murdered many of them, and made one general plunder of their effects, to an immense value.

The frontiers of Pennsylvania, Maryland and Virginia, were immediately over-run with scalping parties, marking their way with blood and devastation wherever they came, and all those examples of savage cruelty, which never fail to accompany an Indian war.

All our out-forts, even at the remotest distances, were attacked about the same time; and the following ones soon fell into the enemies' hands *viz.* Le Boeuf, Venango, Presqu' Isle, on and near Lake Erie; La Bay upon Lake Michigan; St. Joseph's, upon the river of that name; Miamis upon the Miamis River; Ouachtanon upon the Ouabache; Sandusky upon Lake Junundat; and Michilimackinac.

Being but weakly garrisoned, trusting to the security of a general peace so lately established, unable to obtain the least intelligence from the colonies, or from each other, and being separately persuaded by their treacherous and savage assailants, that they had carried every other place before them, it could not be expected that these small posts could hold out long; and the fate of their garrisons is terrible to relate.

The news of their surrender, and the continued ravages of the enemy, struck all America with consternation, and depopulated a great part of our frontiers. We now saw most of those posts, suddenly wrested from us, which had been the great object of the late war, and one of the principal advantages acquired by the peace. Only the forts of Niagara, the Detroit and Fort Pitt, remained in our hands, of all that had been purchased with so much blood and treasure. But these were places of consequence, and we hope it ever will remain an argument of their importance, and of the attention that should be paid to their future support, that they alone continued to awe the whole power of the Indians and balanced the fate of the war between them and us!

These forts, being larger, were better garrisoned and supplied to stand a siege of some than the places that fell. Niagara was not attacked, the enemy judging it too strong.

The officers who commanded the other two deserve the highest honour for the firmness with which they defended them, and the hardships they sustained rather than deliver up places of such importance.

Major Gladwin, in particular, who commanded at the Detroit, had to withstand the united and vigorous attacks of all the nations living upon the Lakes.

The design of this publication, and the materials in my hands, lead me more immediately to speak of the defence and relief of Fort Pitt.

The Indians had early surrounded that place, and cut off all communication from it, even by message. Though they had no cannon, nor understood the methods of a regular siege, yet, with incredible boldness, they posted themselves under the banks of both rivers (Ohio and Monongahela, at the junction of which stands Fort Pitt), by the walls of the fort, and continued as it were buried there, from day to day, with astonishing patience; pouring in an incessant storm of musketry and fire arrows; hoping at length, by famine, by fire, or by harassing out the garrison, to carry their point.

Captain Ecuyer, who commanded there, though he wanted several necessaries for sustaining a siege, and the fortifications had been greatly damaged by the floods, took all the precautions which art and judgement could suggest for the repair of me place, and repulsing the enemy. His garrison, joined by the inhabitants, and surviving traders who had taken refuge there, seconded his efforts with resolution. Their situation was alarming, being remote from all immediate assistance, and having to deal with an enemy from whom they had no mercy to expect.

General Amherst, the commander in chief, not being able to provide in time for the safety of the remote posts, bent his chief attention to the relief of the Detroit, Niagara, and Fort Pitt. The communication with the two former was chiefly by water, from the province of New York; and it was on that account the more easy to throw succours into them. The detachment sent to the Detroit arrived there on the 29th of July, 1763; but Captain Dalyell, who commanded that detachment, and seventy of his men, lost their lives in a rencontre with the Indians near the fort. Previous to this disaster he had passed through Niagara and left a reinforcement there.

Fort Pitt remained all this while in a most critical situation. No account could be obtained from the garrison, nor any relief sent to it, but by a long and tedious land march of near 200 miles beyond the settlements; and through those dangerous passes where the fate of Braddock and others still rises on the imagination.

Colonel Bouquet was appointed to march to the relief of this fort, with a large quantity of military stores and provisions, escorted by the shattered remainder of the 42nd and 77th Regiments, lately returned in a dismal condition from the West Indies, and far from being recovered of their fatigues at the siege of the Havannah. General Amherst, having at that time no other troops to spare, was obliged to employ them in a service which would have required men of the strongest constitution and vigour.

Early orders had been given to prepare a convoy of provisions on the frontiers of Pennsylvania, but such were the universal terror and consternation of the inhabitants, that when Colonel Bouquet arrived at Carlisle, nothing had yet been done. A great number of the plantations had been plundered and burnt, by the savages; many of the mills destroyed, and the full-ripe crops stood waving in the field, ready for the sickle, but the reapers were not to be found!

The greatest part of the county of Cumberland, through which the army had to pass, was deserted, and the roads were covered with distressed families, flying from their settlements, and destitute of all the necessaries of life.

In the midst of that general confusion, the supplies necessary for the expedition became very precarious, nor was it less difficult to procure horses and carriages for the use of the troops.

The commander found that, instead of expecting such supplies from a miserable people, he himself was called by the voice of humanity to bestow on them some share of his own provisions to relieve their present exigency. However, in eighteen days after his arrival at Carlisle, by the prudent and active measures which he pursued, joined to his knowledge of the country, and the diligence of the persons he employed, the convoy and carriages were procured with the assistance of the interior parts of the country, and the army proceeded.

Their march did not abate the fears of the dejected inhabitants. They knew the strength and ferocity of the enemy. They remembered the former defeats even of our best troops and were full of diffidence and apprehensions on beholding the small number and sickly state of the regulars employed in this expedition. Without the least hopes, therefore, of success, they seemed only to wait for the fatal event, which they dreaded, to abandon all the country beyond the Susquehannah.

In such despondency of mind, it is not surprising, that though their whole was at stake, and depended entirely upon the fate of this little army, none of them offered to assist in the defence of the country, by joining the expedition; in which they would have been of infinite service, being in general well acquainted with the woods, and excellent marksmen.

It cannot be contested that the defeat of the regular troops on this occasion, would have left the province of Pennsylvania in particular, exposed to the most imminent danger, from a victorious, daring and barbarous enemy; for (excepting the frontier people of Cumberland county) the bulk of its industrious inhabitants is composed of merchants, tradesmen and farmers, unaccustomed to arms, and without a militia law.

The legislature ordered, indeed, 700 men to be raised for the protection of the frontiers during the harvest; but what dependence could be placed in raw troops, newly raised and undisciplined? Under so many discouraging circumstances, the colonel (deprived of all assistance from the provinces, and having none to expect from the general, who had sent him the last man that could be removed from the hospitals) had nothing else to trust to, but about 500 soldiers of approved courage and resolution indeed, but infirm, and entire strangers to the woods, and to this new kind of war. A number of them were even so weak, as not to be able to march, and sixty were carried in wagons to reinforce the garrisons of the small posts on the communication.

Meanwhile Fort Ligonier, situated beyond the Allegheny Mountains, was in the greatest danger of falling into the hands of the enemy, before the army could reach it. The stockade being very bad, and the garrison extremely weak, they had attacked it vigorously, but had been repulsed by the bravery, and good conduct of Lieutenant Blane who commanded there.

The preservation of that post was of the utmost consequence, on account of its situation and. the quantity of military stores it contained, which if the enemy could have got possession of, would, have enabled them to continue their attack upon Fort Pitt, and reduced the army to the greatest streights. For an object of that importance, every risk was to be run; and the colonel determined to send through the woods, with proper guides, a party of thirty men to join that garrison. They succeeded by forced marches in that hazardous attempt, not having been discovered by the enemy till they came within sight of the fort, into which they threw themselves, after receiving some running shot.

Previous to that reinforcement of regulars, twenty volunteers, all good woodsmen, had been sent to Fort Ligonier by Captain Ourry, who commanded at Fort Bedford another very considerable magazine of provisions, and military stores, the principal and centrical stage between Carlisle and Fort Pitt, being about a hundred miles distance from each. This fort was also in a ruinous condition, and very weakly garrisoned, although the two small intermediate posts, at the crossings of the Juniata and of Stony Creek, had been abandoned to strengthen it.

Here the distressed families, scattered for twelve or fifteen miles round, fled for protection, leaving most of their effects a prey to the savages.

All the necessary precautions were taken by the commanding officer, to prevent surprise, and repel open force, as also to render ineffectual the enemies fire arrows. He armed all the fighting men, who formed two companies of volunteers, and did duty with the garrison till the arrival of two companies of Light Infantry, detached as soon as possible from Colonel Bouquet's little army.

These two magazines being secured, the colonel advanced to the remotest verge of our settlements, where he could receive no sort of intelligence of the number, position, or motions of the enemy. Not even at Fort Bedford, where he arrived with his whole convoy on the 25th of July, for though the Indians did not attempt to attack the fort, they had by this time killed, scalped, and taken eighteen persons in that neighbourhood, and then skulking parties were so spread, that at last no express could escape them.

> This (want of intelligence) is often a very embarrassing circumstance in the conduct of a campaign in America. The Indians had better intelligence, and no sooner were they informed of the march of our army, than they broke up the siege of Fort Pitt, and took the rout by which they knew we were to proceed, resolved to take the first advantageous opportunity of an attack on the march.

In this uncertainty of intelligence under which the colonel laboured, he marched from Fort Bedford the 28th of July, and as soon as he reached Fort Ligonier, he determined very prudently to leave his wagons at that post, and to proceed only with the pack horses. Thus disburdened, the army continued their rout. Before them lay a dangerous defile at Turtle Creek, several miles in length, commanded the whole way by high and craggy hills. This defile he intended to have passed the ensuing night, by a double or forced march; thereby, if possible, to elude the vigilance of so alert an enemy, proposing only to make a short halt in his way, to refresh the troops, at Bushy Run.

When they came within half, a mile of that place, about one in the afternoon, (August 5th, 1763) after an harassing march of seventeen miles, and just as they were expecting to relax from their fatigue, they were suddenly attacked by the Indians, on their advanced guard; which being speedily and firmly supported, the enemy was beat off, and even pursued to a considerable distance.

> But the flight of these barbarians must often be considered as a part of the engagement, (if we may use the expression) rather than a dereliction of the field. The moment the pursuit ended, they returned with renewed vigour to the attack. Several other parties, who had been in ambush in some high grounds which lay along the flanks of the army, now started up at once, and. falling with a resolution

equal to that of their companions, galled our troops with a most obstinate fire.

It was necessary to make a general charge with the whole line to dislodge them from these heights. This charge succeeded; but still the success produced no decisive advantage; for as soon as the savages were driven from one post, they still appeared on another, till by constant reinforcements they were at length able to surround the whole detachment, and attack the convoy which had been left in the rear.

This manoeuvre obliged the main body to fall back in order to protect it. The action, which grew every moment hotter and hotter, now became general. Our troops were attacked on every side; the savages supported their spirit throughout; but the steady behaviour of the English troops, who were not thrown in the least confusion by the very discouraging nature of this service, in the end prevailed; they repulsed the enemy, and drove them from all their posts with fixed bayonets.

The engagement ended only with the day, having continued from one without any intermission.

The ground, on which the action ended, was not altogether inconvenient for an encampment. The convoy and the wounded were in the middle, and the troops, disposed in a circle, encompassed the whole. In this manner, and with little repose, they passed an anxious night, obliged to the strictest vigilance by an enterprising enemy who had surrounded them.

Those who have only experienced the severities and dangers of a campaign in Europe, can scarcely form an idea of what is to be done and endured in an American war. To act in a country cultivated and inhabited, where roads are made, magazines are established, and hospitals provided; where there are good towns to retreat to in case of misfortune; or, at the worst, a generous enemy to yield to, from whom no consolation, but the honour of victory, can be wanting; this may be considered as the exercise of a spirited and adventurous mind, rather than a rigid contest where all is at stake, and mutual destruction the object: and as a contention between rivals for glory, rather than a real struggle between sanguinary enemies. But in an American campaign everything is terrible; the face of the country, the climate, the enemy.

There is no refreshment for the healthy, nor relief for the sick. A vast unhospitable desert, unsafe and treacherous, surrounds them, where victories are not decisive, but defeats are ruinous; and simple death is the least misfortune which can happen to them. This forms a service truly critical, in which all the firmness of the body and. mind is put to the severest trial; and all the exertions of courage and address are called out. If the actions of these rude campaigns are of less dignity, the adventures in them are more interesting to the heart, and more amusing to the imagination, than the events of a regular war.

But to return to the party of English, whom we left in the woods. At the first dawn of light the savages began to declare themselves, all about the camp, at the distance of about 500 yards; and by shouting and yelling in the most horrid manner, quite round that extensive circumference, endeavoured to strike terror by an ostentation of their numbers, and their ferocity. After this alarming preparative, they attacked our forces, and, under the favour of an incessant fire, made several bold attempts to penetrate into the camp. They were repulsed in every attempt, but by no means discouraged from new ones. Our troops, continually victorious, were continually in danger. They were besides extremely fatigued with a long march, and with the equally long action, of the preceding day; and they were distressed to the last degree by a total want of water, much more intolerable than the enemy s fire.

Tied to their convoy, they could not lose sight of it for a moment, without exposing, not only that interesting object, but their wounded men, to fall a prey to the savages, who pressed them on every side. To move was impracticable. Many of the horses were lost, and many of the drivers, stupefied by their fears, hid themselves in the bushes, and were incapable of hearing or obeying orders.

Their situation became extremely critical and perplexing, having experienced that the most lively efforts made no impression upon an enemy, who always gave way when pressed; but who, the moment the pursuit was over, returned with as much alacrity as ever to the attack. Besieged rather than engaged; attacked without interruption, and without decision; able neither to advance nor to retreat, they saw before them the most melancholy prospect of crumbling away by degrees, and entirely perishing without revenge or honour, in the midst of those dreadful deserts. The fate of Braddock was every moment before their eyes; but they were more ably conducted.

The commander was sensible that everything depended upon bringing the savages to a close engagement, and to stand their ground when attacked. Their audaciousness, which had increased with their success, seemed favourable to this design. He endeavoured, therefore, to increase their confidence as much as possible.

For that purpose, he contrived the following stratagem. Our troops were posted on an eminence and formed a circle round their convoy from the preceding night, which order they still retained. Colonel Bouquet gave directions that two companies of his troops, who had been posted in the most advanced situations, should fall within the circle; the troops on the right and left immediately opened their files, and filled up the vacant space, that they might seem to cover their retreat. Another company of light infantry, with one of grenadiers, were ordered to 'lie in ambuscade,' to support the two first companies of grenadiers, who moved on the feigned retreat, and were intended to begin the real attack. The dispositions were well made, and the plan executed without the least confusion.

The savages gave entirely into the snare. The thin line of troops, which took possession of the ground which the two companies of light foot had left, being brought in nearer to the centre of the circle, the barbarians mistook those motions for a retreat, abandoned the woods which covered them, hurried headlong on, and advancing with the most daring intrepidity, galled, the English troops with their heavy fire. But at the very moment when, certain of success, they thought themselves masters of the camp, the two first companies made a sudden turn, and sallying out from a part of the hill, which could not be observed, fell furiously upon their right flank.

The savages, though they found themselves disappointed and exposed, preserved their recollection, and resolutely returned the fire which they had received. Then it was the superiority of combined strength and discipline appeared. On the second charge they could no longer sustain the irresistible shock of the regular troops, who rushing upon them, killed many, and put the rest to flight.

At the instant when the savages betook themselves to flight, the other two companies, which had been ordered to support the first, rose 'from ambuscade,' marched to the enemy, and gave them their full fire. This accomplished their defeat. The four companies now united, did not give them time to look behind them, but pursued the enemy till they were totally dispersed.

The other bodies of the savages attempted nothing. They were kept in awe during the engagement by the rest of the British troops, who were so posted as to be ready to fall on them upon the least motion. Having been witnesses to the defeat of their companions, without any effort to support or assist them, they at length followed their example and fled.

This judicious and successful manoeuvre rescued the party from the most imminent danger. The victory secured

the field and cleared all the adjacent woods. But still the march was so difficult, and the army had suffered so much, and so many horses were lost, that before they were able to proceed, they were reluctantly obliged to destroy such part of their convoy of provisions as they could not carry with them for want of horses. Being lightened by this sacrifice, they proceeded to Bushy Run, where finding water, they encamped.
(The above quotation is from the writer already mentioned, and seems so accurately and elegantly drawn up, from the account of this engagement, sent to his Majesty's ministers, that nothing better can be inserted in its room. There are but one or two small mistakes in it, which are here corrected.)

A plan of this engagement is annexed, and it was thought the more necessary here to insert a particular account of it, as the new manoeuvres and skilful conduct of the commander, seem to have been the principal means, not only of preserving his army in the most critical situation, but likewise of ensuring them a complete victory.

★★★★★★

Another reason for being so particular in this account, is that the military papers annexed to this work, and the plan for carrying on any future war with the Indians, were composed upon the experience of this engagement, by an officer long employed in the service he describes. His own improvement was his principal motive in the composition of them; but being told that they might convey many useful hints to others and be of much service if laid before the public, he was pleased, upon my request, freely to communicate them to me for that purpose.

★★★★★★

The enemy lost about sixty men on this occasion, some of them their chief warriors; which they reputed a very severe stroke. They had likewise many wounded in the pursuit. The English lost about fifty men and had about sixty wounded.

The savages, thus signally defeated in all their attempts to cut off this reinforcement upon its march, began to retreat with the utmost precipitation to their remote settlements, wholly giving up their designs against Fort Pitt; at which place Colonel Bouquet arrived safe with his convoy, four days after the action; receiving no further molestation on the road, except a few scattered shot from a disheartened and flying enemy.

Here the colonel was obliged to put an end to the operations of this campaign, not having a sufficient force to pursue the enemy beyond the Ohio and take advantage of the victory obtained over them; nor having any reason to expect a timely reinforcement from the provinces in their distressed situation. He was therefore forced to content himself with supplying Fort Pitt, and other places on the communication, with provisions, ammunition and stores; stationing his small army to the best advantage he could, against the approach of winter.

The transactions of the succeeding campaign, will be the subject of the following work, and we shall conclude this introduction, by shewing the sense which his Majesty was pleased to entertain, of the conduct and bravery of the officers and army, on this trying occasion.

Headquarters, New York,<br>Jan. 5, 1764.

Orders.

His Majesty has been graciously pleased to signify to the commander in chief, his royal approbation of the conduct and bravery of Colonel Bouquet and the officers and troops under his command, in the two actions of the 5th and 6th of August; in which, notwithstanding the many circumstances of difficulty and distress they laboured under, and the unusual spirit and resolution of the Indians, they repelled, and defeated the repeated attacks of the savages, and conducted their convoy sale to Fort Pitt.

Signed

Moncreif,<br>Major of Brigade.

To Colonel Bouquet,
or officer commanding at Fort Pitt.

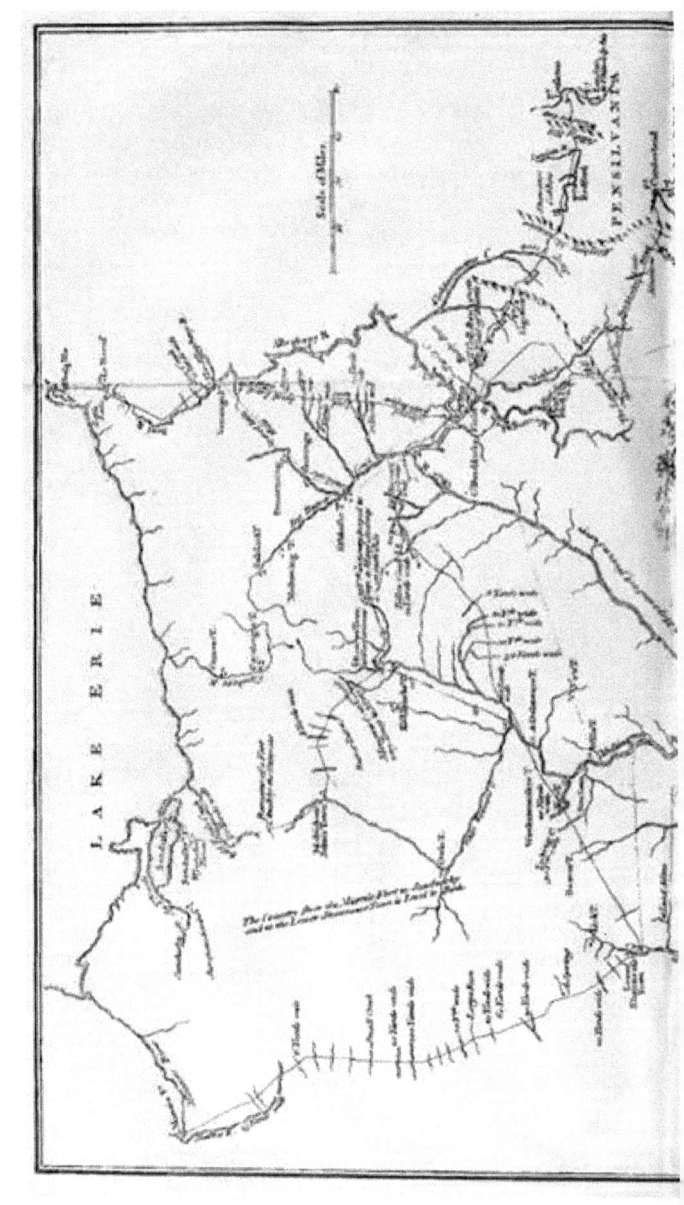

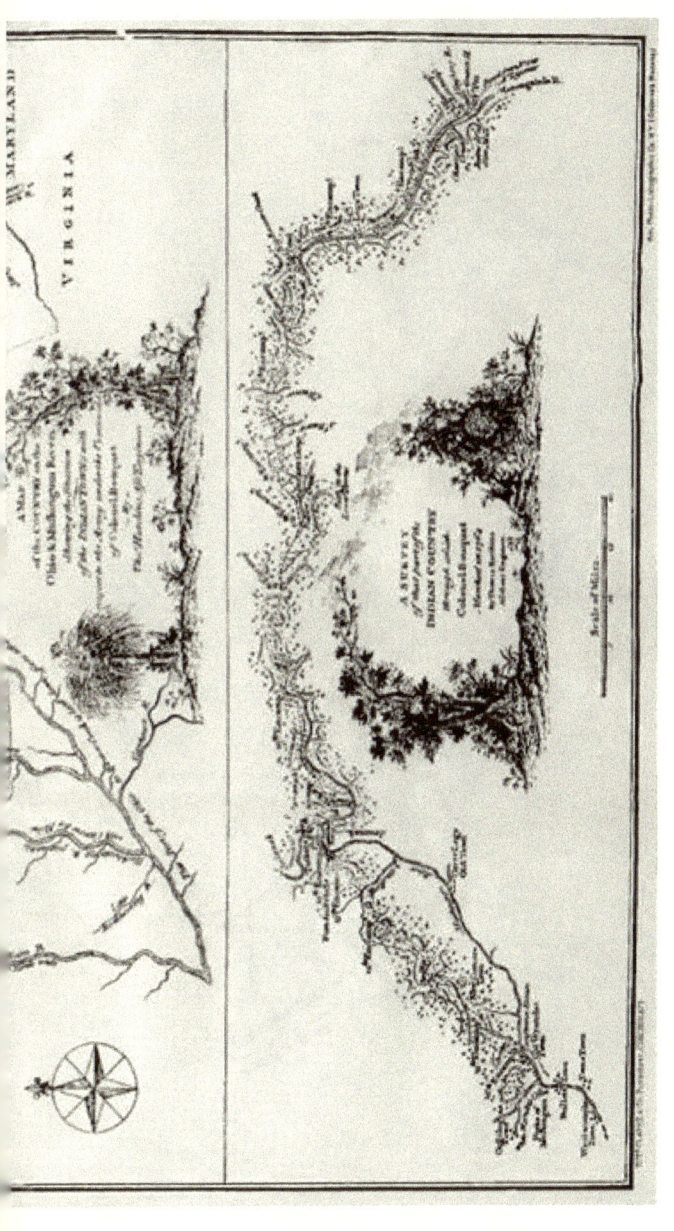

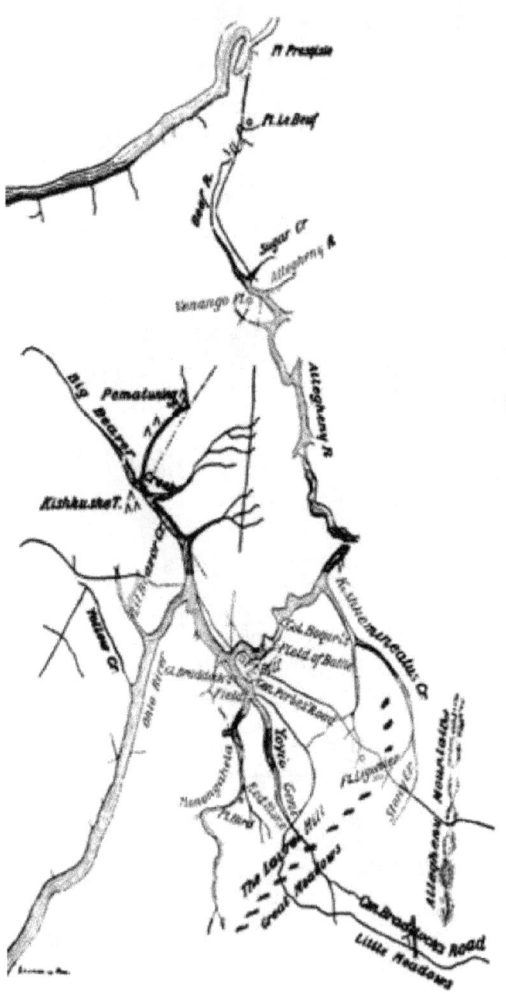

# Colonel Bouquet's Expedition Against the Ohio Indians in the Year 1764

In the preceding introduction, some account hath been given of the sudden, treacherous and unprovoked attack, made by the Indians upon the frontiers of Pennsylvania, Maryland, and Virginia, soon after the publication of the general Peace, at a time when we were but just beginning to respire from our former calamities, and looked for an approach of quiet on every side. The principal transactions of the campaign 1763 have likewise been briefly recapitulated, and the reader informed by what means the editor became possessed of the valuable papers, which have enabled him to bring the history of this Indian war to a conclusion and furnished the materials of the following sheets.

Colonel Bouquet, as before mentioned, not having a sufficient number of troops to garrison the different posts, under his command, and at the same time to cross the Ohio and take advantage of the dejection into which he had thrown the enemy, by the defeat at Bushy Run, was obliged to restrain his operations to the supplying the forts with provisions, ammunition and other necessaries.

In the execution of this service, he received no annoyance from the enemy, for they now saw themselves not only forced to give up their designs against Fort Pitt; but retreating beyond the Ohio, they deserted their former towns, and abandoned all the country between Presque Isle and Sanduski; not thinking themselves safe till they arrived at Muskingum.

Here they began to form new settlements and remained quiet during the winter. But, in the meantime, having supplied themselves with powder, &c. from the French traders, (and now nattering themselves that the great distance of their settlements would render them inaccessible to our troops) the ensuing spring 1764 presented these savage enemies afresh on our frontiers; ravaging and murdering with their usual

To chastise them for their perfidy, General Gage resolved to attack them on two different sides, and to force them from our frontiers; by carrying the war into the heart of their own country. With this view, he destined a corps of troops to proceed under Colonel Bradstreet, to act against the Wyandottes, Ottawas, Chipwas and other nations, living upon or near the lakes; while another corps, under the command of Colonel Bouquet, should attack the Delawares, Shawanese, Mingoes, Mohickons, and other nations, between the Ohio and the lakes.

These two corps were to act in concert; and as that of Colonel Bradstreet could be ready much sooner than the other, he was to proceed to Detroit, Michilimackinac and other places. On his return he was to encamp and remain at Sanduski, to awe, by that position, the numerous tribes of western Indians, so as to prevent their sending any assistance to the Ohio Indians, while Colonel Bouquet should execute his plan of attacking them in the heart of their settlements.

Colonel Bouquet's expedition was to proceed altogether by land and was on that account attended with great difficulties. His men were to penetrate through a continued depth of woods, and a savage unexplored country; without roads, without posts, and without a retreat if they failed of success. When once engaged in these deserts, they had no convoy, nor any kind of assistance to expect. Everything was to be carried with them—their ammunition, baggage, tools, stores, and provisions necessary for the troops during the whole expedition. And besides, they were liable to many embarrassments, and difficulties which no prudence could foresee, scarce any caution prevent; so that, in this account, sundry things, which, in the usual method of conducting military operations, might not be thought worthy of detail, may nevertheless be found highly serviceable to those who may afterwards be employed in this species of war, which is new to Europeans, who must submit to be instructed in it by experience, and in many articles even by the savages themselves.

Part of the 42nd and 60th Regiments were ordered on this expedition and were to be joined by two hundred friendly Indians, and the troops required of Virginia and Pennsylvania. The Indians never came, and the Virginians pleaded their inability to raise men, having already in pay about 700 militia for the defence of their own frontier. In Pennsylvania, a bill for raising 1000 men was passed May 30th; but, with the utmost diligence that could be used, the number could not be completed till the beginning of August.

On the 5th of that month, the men being assembled at Carlisle, one hundred and eighteen miles to the westward of Philadelphia, Governor Penn, who had accompanied Colonel Bouquet to that place, acquainted the two Pennsylvania battalions with the necessity we were laid under of chastising the Indians:

> For their repeated and unprovoked barbarities on the inhabitants of the Province; a just resentment of which, added to a remembrance of the loyalty and courage of our provincial troops on former occasions, he did not doubt, would animate them to do honour to their country; and that they could not but hope to be crowned with success, as they were to be united with the same regular troops, and under the same able commander, who had by themselves, on that very day, the memorable 5th of August in the preceding year, sustained the repeated attacks of the savages, and obtained a complete victory over them.

He also reminded them of:

> The exemplary punishments that would be inflicted on the grievous crime of desertion, if any of them were capable of so far forgetting their solemn oath and duty to their king and country, as to be involved in it.

Colonel Bouquet then assumed the command of the regular and provincial troops; and the four following days were spent in the necessary preparations for their march; the colonel giving the most express orders to the officers and men to observe strict discipline, and not to commit the least violation of the civil rights or peace of the inhabitants—He, at the same time, made the most prudent regulations for a safe and commodious carriage of the baggage, taking care to rid himself of all unnecessary encumbrances.

The 13th of August this small army got to Fort Loudoun; but notwithstanding all the precautions taken to prevent desertion, the Pennsylvania troops were now reduced to about 700 men. The colonel was therefore under a necessity to apply to the government of that province to enable him to complete their number to the full complement; which was generously granted by a resolve of the Governor and Commissioners August 16th; and the army advancing now beyond the settled parts of Pennsylvania, he made application to the colony of Virginia, where (under the countenance of Governor Fauquier) the men wanted were soon raised, and joined the army at Pittsburg, about the latter end of September.

Nothing material happened in their march, from Fort Loudoun to Fort Pitt, (formerly Fort Duquesne) on the Ohio, three hundred and twenty miles west from Philadelphia; at which place Colonel Bouquet arrived the 17th of September.

During this interval, several large convoys were forwarded under strong escorts; and though the enemy continued their ravages all that time on the frontiers, they durst not attack any of those convoys, which all arrived safe at Fort Pitt.

While Colonel Bouquet was at Fort Loudoun, he received dispatches by express from Colonel Bradstreet, dated from Presque Isle August 14th, acquainting him that he (Colonel Bradstreet) had concluded a peace with the Delawares and Shawanese; but Colonel Bouquet perceiving clearly that they were not sincere in their intentions, as they continued their murders and depredations, he determined to prosecute his plan without remission, till he should receive further instructions from

General Gage; who, upon the same principles, refused to ratify the treaty, and renewed his orders to both armies to attack the enemy.

About the time of Colonel Bouquet's arrival at Fort Pitt, ten Indians appeared on the north side of the Ohio, desiring a conference; which stratagem the savages had made use of before, to obtain intelligence of our numbers and intentions. Three of the party consented, though with apparent reluctance, to come over to the fort; and. as they could give no satisfactory reason for their visit, they were detained as spies, and their associates lied back to their towns.

On the 20th of September Colonel Bouquet sent one of the above three Indians after them with a message, in substance as follows—

> I have received an account from Colonel Bradstreet that your nations had begged for peace, which he had consented to grant, upon assurance that you had recalled all your warriors from our frontiers; and in consequence thereof, I would not have proceeded against your towns, if I had not heard that, in open violation of your engagements, you have since murdered several of our people. As soon as the rest of the army joins me, which I expect immediately, I was therefore determined to have attacked you, as a people whose promises can no more be relied on. But I will put it once more in your power to save yourselves and your families from total destruction, by giving us satisfaction for the hostilities committed against us.
>
> And first you are to leave the path open for my expresses from hence to Detroit; and as I am now to send two men with dispatches to Colonel Bradstreet who commands on the lakes, I desire to know whether you will send two of your people with them to bring them safe back with an answer? And if they receive any injury either in going or coming, or if the letters are taken from them, I will immediately put the Indians now in my power to death and will shew no mercy for the future to any of your nations

Council meeting between Indians and Colonel Bouquet Oct. 1764

that shall fall into my hands. I allow you ten days to have my letters delivered at Detroit, and ten days, to bring me back an answer.

He added that:

> He had lately had it in his power, while they remained on the other side of the river, to have put their whole party to death, which punishment they had deserved by their former treachery; and that if they did not improve the clemency now offered to them, by returning back as soon as possible with all their prisoners, they might expect to feel the full weight of a just vengeance and resentment.

We have been the more particular in our account of this first transaction with the Indians; because the colonel's firm and determined conduct in opening the campaign, had happy effects in the prosecution of it, and shews by what methods these faithless savages are to be best reduced to reason.

On the 1st of October, two of the Six Nation tribes, an Onondago and Oneida Indian, came to Fort Pitt, and under colour of our ancient friendship with them, and their pretended regard to the English, endeavoured to dissuade the colonel from proceeding with the army. They told him that his force was not sufficient to withstand the power of the numerous nations through whose country he was to pass and assured him that if he would wait a little, they would all come and make peace with him; at the same time recommending it particularly to him to send back the two Indians detained as spies. These little arts being clearly made use of to spin out the season till the approach of winter should render it impossible to proceed, they made but little impression. He told them that he could not depend on the promises of the Delawares and Shawanese; and was determined to proceed to Tuscarowas, where, if they had anything to say, he would hear them.

In the meantime, he was using the utmost diligence to prepare for his march and was obliged to enforce the severest discipline. One woman belonging to each corps, and two nurses for the general hospital, were all that were permitted. to follow the army. The other women in the camp, and those unnecessary in the garrison, were ordered immediately down the country into the settlements. Two soldiers were shot for desertion, an example which became absolutely necessary to suppress a crime which, in such an expedition, would have been attended with fatal consequences, by weakening an army already too small.

Colonel Bouquet, having at length, with great difficulty, collected his troops, formed his magazines, and provided for the safety of the posts he was to leave behind him, was ready on the 2nd of October to proceed from Fort Pitt, with about 1500 men, including drivers and other necessary followers of the army.

As a just idea of the conduct of this expedition, and the great caution taken to prevent surprise, will be best obtained from the order of march, we shall here insert it, and an accurate draught, taken from actual surveys, of the road and adjacent country, through which the army passed.

The colonel, expressing the greatest confidence in the bravery of the troops, told them, he did not doubt but this war would soon be ended "under God, to their own honour, and the future safety of their country, provided the men were strictly obedient to orders, and guarded against the surprises and sudden attacks of a treacherous enemy, who never dared to face British troops in an open held; that the distance of the enemy's towns, and the clearing roads to them, must necessarily require a considerable time; that the troops in those deserts, had no other supplies to expect but the ammunition and provisions they carried with them; and that therefore the utmost care and frugality would be necessary in the use of them." He published the severest penalties against those who should be found guilty of stealing or embezzling any part of them, and ordered his march, in the following manner.—

> A corps of Virginia volunteers advanced before the whole; detaching three scouting parties. (These were the men raised in Virginia, to complete the Pennsylvania troops, and were in the pay of the last-mentioned province.) One of them, furnished with a guide, marched in the centre

path, which the army was to follow. The other two extended themselves in a line abreast, on the right and left of the aforesaid party, to reconnoitre the woods.

Under cover of this corps, the axe-men, consisting of all the artificers, and two companies of light infantry, followed in three divisions, under the direction of the chief engineer, to clear three different paths, in which the troops and the convoy followed, *viz.*—

The front face of the square, composed of part of the 42nd Regiment, marched in a column, two deep, in the centre path.

The right face of the square, composed of the remainder of the 42nd and of the 60th Regiment, marched in a single file in the right-hand path.

The first battalion of Pennsylvanians composed the left face, marching in like manner in the path to the left of the centre.

The *corps de reserve*, composed of two platoons of grenadiers, followed the right and left faces of the square.

The 2nd battalion of Pennsylvanians formed the rear face of the square, and followed the *corps de reserve*, each in a single file, on the right- and left-hand paths; all these troops covering the convoy, which moved in the centre path.

A party of light horsemen marched behind the rear face of the square, followed by another corps of Virginia volunteers, forming the rear-guard.

The Pennsylvania volunteers, dividing themselves equally, and marching in a single file, at a proper distance, flanked the right and left faces of the square.

This was the general order of march. Nor was less attention paid to particular matters of a subordinate nature. The ammunition and tools were placed in the rear of the first column, or front face of the square, followed by the officers' baggage, and tents. The oxen and sheep came after the baggage in separate droves, properly guarded. The provisions came next to the baggage, in four divisions, or brigades of pack-horses, each conducted by a horse-master.

The troops were ordered to observe the most profound silence, and the men to march at two yards distance from one another. When the line or any part of it halted, the whole were to face outwards; and if attacked on their march, they were to halt immediately, ready to form the square when ordered. The light horse were then to march into the square, with the cattle, provisions, ammunition and baggage. Proper dispositions were likewise made in case of an attack in the night; and for encampments, guards, communications between the sentries, signals, and the like.

Things being thus settled, the army decamped from Fort Pitt on Wednesday, October 3rd, and marched about one mile and an half over a rich level country, with stately timber, to camp No. 2, a strong piece of ground, pleasantly situated, with plenty of water and food for cattle.

*Thursday October 4th*, having proceeded about two miles, they came to the Ohio, at the beginning of the narrows, and from thence followed the course of the river along a flat gravelly beach, about six miles and a quarter; with two islands on their left, the lowermost about six miles long, with a rising ground running across, and gently sloping on both sides to its banks, which are high and upright. At the lower end of this island, the army left the river, marching through good land, broken with small hollows to camp No. 3; this day's march being nine miles and a quarter.

*Friday October 5th*. In this day's march the army passed through Loggs-town, situated seventeen miles and an half, fifty seven perches, by the path, from Fort Pitt. This place was noted before the last war for the great trade carried on there by the English and French; but its inhabitants, the Shawanese and Delawares, abandoned it in the year 1750. The lower town extended about sixty perches over a rich bottom to the foot of a low steep ridge, on the summit of which, near the declivity, stood the upper town, commanding a most agreeable prospect over the lower, and quite across the Ohio, which is about 500 yards wide here, and by its majestic easy current adds much to the beauty of the place. Proceeding beyond Loggs-town, through a fine country, interspersed with hills and rich valleys, watered by many rivulets, and covered with stately timber, they came to camp No. 4; on a level piece of ground, with a thicket in the rear, a small precipice round the front, with a run of water at the foot, and good food for cattle. This day's march was nine miles, one half, and fifty-three perches.

*Saturday October 6th,* at about three miles distance from this camp, they came again to the Ohio, pursuing its course half a mile farther, and men turning on, over a steep ridge, they crossed, Big Beaver Creek, which is twenty perches wide, the ford stony and pretty deep. It runs through a rich vale, with a pretty strong current, its banks high, the upland adjoining it very good, the timber tall and young—About a mile below its confluence with the Ohio, stood formerly a large town, on a steep bank, built by the French of square logs, with stone chimneys, for some of the Shawanese, Delaware and Mingo tribes, who abandoned it in the year 1758, when the French deserted Fort Duquesne. Near the fording of Beaver Creek also stood about seven houses, which were deserted and destroyed by the Indians, after their defeat at Bushy Run, when they forsook all their remaining settlements in this part of the country, as has been mentioned above.

About two miles before the army came to Beaver Creek, one of our people who had been made prisoner by six Delawares about a week before, near Fort Bedford, having made his escape from them, came and informed the colonel that these Indians had the day before fallen in with the army, but kept themselves concealed, being surprised at our numbers. Two miles beyond Beaver Creek, by two small springs, was seen the skull of a child, that had been fixed on a pole by the Indians. The tracts of fifteen Indians were this day discovered. The camp No. 5 is seven miles one quarter and fifty-seven perches from big Beaver Creek; the whole march of this day being about twelve miles.

*Sunday 7th October,* passing a high ridge, they had a fine prospect of an extensive country to the right, which in general appeared level, with abundance of tall timber. The camp No. 6 lies at the foot of a steep descent, in a rich valley, on a strong ground, three sides thereof surrounded by a hollow, and on the fourth side a small hill, which was occupied by a detached guard. This day s march was six miles sixty-five perches.

*Monday 8th October,* the army crossed little Beaver Creek, and. one of its branches. This creek is eight perches wide, with a good ford, the country about it interspersed with hills, rivulets and rich valleys, like that described above. Camp No. 7 lies by a small run on the side of a hill, commanding the ground about it, and is distant eleven miles one quarter and forty-nine perches from the last encampment.

*Tuesday October 9th.* In this day s march, the path divided into two branches, that to the south-west leading to the lower towns upon the Muskingum. In the forks of the path stand several trees painted by the Indians, in a hieroglyphic manner, denoting the number of wars in which they have been engaged, and the particulars of their success in prisoners and scalps. The camp No. 8 lies on a run, and level piece of ground, with Yellow Creek close on the left, and a rising ground near the rear of the right face. The path after the army left the forks was so brushy and entangled, that they were obliged to cut all the way before them, and also to lay several bridges, in order to make it passable for the horses; so that this day they proceeded only five miles, three-quarters and seventy perches.

*Wednesday 10th.* Marched one mile with Yellow Creek on the left at a small distance all the way and crossed it at a good ford, fifty feet wide; proceeding through an alternate succession of small hills and rich vales, finely watered with rivulets, to camp No. 9, seven miles and sixty perches in the whole.

*Thursday 11th.* Crossed a branch of Muskingum River about fifty feet wide, the country much the same as that described above, discovering a good deal of free stone. The camp No. 10. had this branch of the river parallel to its left face and lies ten miles one quarter and forty perches from the former encampment.

*Friday 12th.* Keeping the aforesaid creek on their left, they marched through much fine land, watered with small rivers and springs; proceeding likewise through several savannahs or cleared spots, which are by nature extremely beautiful; the second which they passed being, in particular, one continued plain of near two miles, with a fine rising ground forming a semicircle around the right hand side, and a pleasant stream of water at about a quarter of a mile distant on the left. The camp No. 11. has the above-mentioned branch of Muskingum on the left, and is distant ten miles and three quarters from the last encampment.

*Saturday 13th.* Crossed Nemenshehelas Creek, about fifty feet wide, a little above where it empties itself into the aforesaid branch of Muskingum, having in their way a pleasant prospect over a large plain, for near two miles on the left. A little further, they came to another small river which they crossed about fifty perches above where it empties into the said branch of the Muskingum. Here a high ridge on the right, and the creek close on the left, form a narrow defile about seventy perches long. Passing afterwards over a very rich bottom, they came to the main branch of Muskingum, about seventy yards wide, with a good ford.

A little below and above the forks of this river is Tuscarowas, a place exceedingly beautiful by situation, the lands rich on both sides of the river; the country on the north-west side being an entire level plain, upwards of five miles in circumference. From the ruined houses appearing here, the Indians who inhabited the place and are now with the Delawares, are supposed to have had about one hundred and fifty warriors. This camp No. 12. is distant eight miles nineteen perches from the former.

*Sunday 14th.* The army remained in camp; and two men who had been dispatched by Colonel Bouquet from Fort Pitt, with letters for Colonel Bradstreet, returned and reported:

That, within a few miles of this place, they had been made prisoners by the Delawares, and carried to one of their towns sixteen miles from hence, where they were kept, till the savages, knowing of the arrival of the army here, set them at liberty, ordering them to acquaint the colonel that the head men of the Delawares and Shawanese were coming as soon as possible to treat of peace with him.

*Monday 15th.* The army moved two miles forty perches further down the Muskingum to camp No. 13, situated on a very high bank, with the river at the foot of it, which is upwards of 100 yards wide at tins place, with a fine level country at some distance from its banks, producing stately timber, free from underwood, and plenty or food for cattle.

The day following, six Indians came to inform the colonel that all their chiefs were assembled about eight miles from the camp, and were ready to treat with him of peace, which they were earnestly desirous of obtaining. He returned for answer that lie would meet them the next day in a bower at some distance from the camp. In the meantime, he ordered a small stockaded fort to be built to deposit provisions for the use of the troops on their return; and to lighten the convoy.

As several large bodies of Indians were now within a few miles of the camp, whose former instances of treachery, although they now declared they came for peace, made it prudent to trust nothing to their intentions, the strictest orders were repeated to prevent a surprise.

*Wednesday 17th.* The colonel, with most of the regular troops, Virginia volunteers and light horse, marched from the camp to the bower erected for the congress. And soon after the troops were stationed, so as to appear to the best advantage, the Indians arrived, and were conducted to the bower. Being seated, they began, in a short time, to smoak their pipe or *calumet*, agreeable to their custom. This ceremony being over, their speakers laid down their pipes, and opened their pouches, wherein were their strings and belts of *wampum*. The Indians present were:

Senecas.

Kiyashuta, chief with 15 warriors.

Delawares.

Custaloga, chief of the Wolfe tribe, Beaver, chief of the Turky tribe, with twenty warriors.

Shawanese.

Keissinautchtha, a chief, and six warriors.

Kiyashuta, Turtle Heart, Custaloga and Beaver, were the speakers.

The general substance of what they had to offer, consisted in excuses for their late treachery and misconduct, throwing the blame on the rashness of their young men and the nations living to the westward of them, suing for peace in the most abject manner, and promising severally to deliver up all their prisoners. After they had concluded, the colonel promised to give them an answer the next day, and then dismissed them, the army returning to the camp.—The badness of the weather, however, prevented his meeting them again till the 20th, when he spoke to them in substance as follows, *viz.*

> That their pretences to palliate their guilt by throwing the blame on the western nations, and the rashness of their young men, were weak and frivolous, as it was in our power to have protected them against all these nations, if they had solicited our assistance, and that it was their own duty to have chastised their young men when they did wrong, and not to suffer themselves to be directed by them.

He recapitulated to them many instances of their former perfidy:

> Their killing or captivating the traders who had been sent among them at their own request, and plundering their effects;—their attacking Fort Pitt, which had been built with their express consent, their murdering four men that had been sent on a public message to them, thereby violating the customs held sacred among all nations, however barbarous;—their attacking the King's troops last year in

the woods, and after being defeated in that attempt, falling upon our frontiers, where they had continued to murder our people to this day, &c.

He told them how treacherously they had violated even their late engagements with Colonel Bradstreet, to whom they had promised to deliver up their prisoners by the 10th of September last, and to recall all their warriors from the frontiers, which they had been so far from complying with, that the prisoners still remained in their custody, and some of their people were even now continuing their depreciations; adding, that these things which he had mentioned, were only "a small part of their numberless murders and breaches of faith; and that their conduct had always been equally perfidious." He said:

You have promised at every former treaty, as you do now, that you would deliver up all your prisoners, and have received every time, on that account, considerable presents, but have never complied with that or any other engagement. I am now to tell you, therefore, that we will be no longer imposed upon by your promises. This army shall not leave your country till you have fully complied with every condition that is to precede my treaty with you.

I have brought with me the relations of the people you have massacred or taken prisoners. They are impatient for revenge; and it is with great difficulty that I can protect you against their just resentment, which is only restrained by the assurances given them that no peace shall ever be concluded till you have given us full satisfaction.—

Your former allies, the Ottawas, Chipwas, Wyandottes, and others, have made their peace with us. The Six Nations have joined us against you. We now surround you, having possession of all the waters of the Ohio, the Mississippi, the Miamis, and the lakes. All the French living in those parts are now subjects of Great Britain and dare no longer assist you. It is therefore in our power totally to extirpate you from being a people—But the English are a merciful and generous nation, averse to shed the blood, even of their most cruel enemies; and if it was possible that you could convince us, that you sincerely repent of your past perfidy, and that we could depend on your good behaviour for the future, you might yet hope for mercy and peace—If I find that you faithfully execute the following preliminary conditions, I will not treat you with the severity you deserve.

I give you twelve days from this date to deliver into my hands at Wakautamike all the prisoners in your possession, without any exception; Englishmen, Frenchmen, women and children; whether adopted in your tribes, married, or living amongst you under any denomination and pretence whatsoever, together with all negroes. And you are to furnish the said prisoners with cloathing, provisions, and horses, to carry them to Fort Pitt.

When you have fully complied with these conditions, you shall then know on what terms you may obtain the peace you sue for.

This speech made an impression on the minds of the savages, which, it is hoped, will not soon be eradicated. The firm, and determined spirit with which the colonel delivered himself, their consciousness of the aggravated injuries they had done us, and the view of the same commander and army that had so severely chastised them at Bushy Run the preceding year, now advanced into the very heart of their remote settlements, after penetrating through wildernesses which they had deemed impassable by regular troops—all these things contributed to bend the haughty temper of the savages to the lowest degree of abasement; so that even their speeches seem to exhibit but few specimens of that strong and ferocious eloquence, which their inflexible spirit of independency has on former occasions inspired.

And though it is not to be doubted, if an opportunity had offered, but they would have fallen upon our army with their usual fierceness, yet when they saw the vigilance and spirit of our troops were such, that they could neither be attacked nor surprised with any prospect of success, their spirits seemed to revolt from the one extreme of insolent boldness, to the other of abject timidity.

And happy will it be for them and for us, if the instances of our humanity and mercy, which they experienced in hat critical situation, shall make as lasting impressions on their savage dispositions, as it is believed the instances of our bravery and power have done; so that they may come to unite, with their fear of the latter, a love of the former; and have their minds gradually opened, by such examples, to the mild dictates of peace and civility.

The reader, it is to be hoped, will readily excuse this digression, if it should be thought one. I now resume our narrative. The two Delaware chiefs, at the close of their speech on the 17th, delivered eighteen white prisoners, and eighty-three small sticks, expressing the number of other prisoners which they had in their possession and promised to bring in as soon as possible. None of the Shawanese Kings appeared at the congress, and Keissinautchtha their deputy declined, speaking until the colonel had answered. the Delawares, and then with a dejected sullenness he promised, in behalf of his nation, that they would submit to the terms prescribed to the other tribes.

The colonel however, determined to march farther into their country, knowing that the presence of his army would be the best security for the performance of their promises; and required some of each nation to attend him in his march.

Kiyashuta addressed the several nations, before their departure:

> Desiring them to be strong in complying with their engagements, that they might wipe away the reproach of their former breach of faith, and convince their brothers the English, that they could speak the truth; adding that he would conduct the army to the place appointed for receiving the prisoners.

*Monday October 22nd.* The army, attended by the Indian deputies, marched nine miles to camp No. 14, crossing Margaret's Creek about fifty feet wide. The day following, they proceeded sixteen miles one quarter and seventy seven perches farther to camp No. 15, and halted there one day.

*Thursday 25th.* They marched six miles, one half and sixteen perches to camp No. 16, situated within a mile of the Forks of Muskingum; and this place was fixed upon instead of Wakautamike, as the most central and convenient place to receive the prisoners; for the principal Indian towns now lay around them, distant from seven to twenty miles; excepting only the lower Shawanese town situated on Scioto River, which was about eighty miles; so that from this place the army had it in their power to awe all the enemy's settlements and destroy their towns, if they should not punctually fulfil the engagements they had entered into.

Four redoubts were built here opposite to the four angles of the camp; the ground in the front was cleared, a store-house for the provisions erected, and likewise a house to receive, and treat of peace with, the Indians, when they should return. Three houses with separate apartments were also raised for the reception of the captives of the respective provinces, and proper officers appointed to take charge of them, with a matron to attend the women and children; so that with the officers' mess houses, ovens, &c. this camp had the appearance of a little town in which the greatest order and regularity were observed.

*Saturday 27th.* A messenger arrived from King Custaloga, informing that he was on his way with his prisoners, and also a messenger from the lower Shawanese towns of the like import. The colonel, however, having no reason to suspect the latter nation of backwardness, sent one of their own people, desiring them:

> To be punctual as to the time fixed to provide a sufficient quantity of provisions to subsist the prisoners; to bring the letters wrote to him last winter by the French commandant at Fort Chartres, which some of their people had stopped ever since; adding that, as their nation had expressed some uneasiness at our not shaking hands with them, they were to know that the English never took their

enemies by the hand, before peace was finally concluded.

The day following the Shawanese messenger returned, saying that when he had proceeded as far as Wakautamike, the chief of that town undertook to proceed with the message himself, and desired the other to return and. acquaint the English that all his prisoners were ready, and he was going to the lower towns to hasten theirs.

*October 28th*.Peter the Caughnawaga chief, and twenty Indians of that nation arrived from Sanduski, with a letter from Colonel Bradstreet, in answer to one which Colonel Bouquet had sent to him from Fort Pitt, by two of the Indians who first spoke to him in favour of the Shawanese, as hath been already mentioned. The substance of Colonel Bradstreet's letter was that:

> He had settled nothing with the Shawanese and Delawares, nor received any prisoners from them.—That he had acquainted all the Indian nations, as far as the Illinois, the bay, &c. with the instructions he had received from General Gage, respecting the peace he had lately made; that he had been in Sanduski Lake and up the river, as far as navigable for Indian canoes, for near a month; but that he found impossible to stay longer in these parts; absolute necessity obliging him to turn off the other way, &c.

Colonel Bradstreet, without doubt, did all which circumstances would permit, in his department; but his not being able to remain at Sanduski, agreeable to the original plan, till matters. were finally settled with the Ohio Indians, would have been an unfavourable incident, if Colonel Bouquet had not now had the chiefs of sundry tribes with him, and was so far advanced into the Indian country, that they thought it advisable to submit to the conditions imposed upon them.

The Caughnawagas reported that the Indians on the lakes had delivered but few of their prisoners; that the Ottawas had killed a great part of theirs, and the other nations had either done the same, or else kept them.

From this time to November 9th, was chiefly spent in sending and receiving messages to and from the Indian towns, relative to the prisoners, who were now coming into the camp one day after another in small parties, as the different nations arrived in whose possession they had been. The colonel kept so steadfastly to this article of having every prisoner delivered, that when the Delaware kings, Beaver and Custaloga, had brought in all theirs except twelve, which they promised to bring in a few days, he refused to shake hands or have the least talk with them, while a single captive remained among them.

By the 9th of November, most of the prisoners were arrived that could be expected this season, amounting to 206 in the whole, (Virginians, Males 32, Females and Children 58; Pennsylvanians, Males 49, Females and Children 67); besides about 100 more in possession of the Shawanese, which they promised to deliver the following spring. Mr. Smallman, formerly a major in the Pennsylvania troops, who had been taken last summer near Detroit by the Wyandottes, and delivered to the Shawanese, was among the number of those whom they now brought in and informed the colonel that the reason of their not bringing the remainder of their prisoners, was that many of their principal men, to whom they belonged, were gone to trade with the French, and would not return for six weeks; but that every one of their nation who were at home, had either brought or sent theirs.

He further said that, on the army's first coming into the country; it had been reported among the Shawanese that our intention was to destroy them all, on which they had resolved to kill their prisoners and fight us; that a French trader who was with them, and had many barrels of powder and ball, made them a present of the whole, as soon as they had come to this resolution; but that, happily for the poor captives, just as the Shawanese were preparing to execute this tragedy, they received the colonel's message, informing them that his intentions were only to receive the prisoners and to make peace with, them on the same terms he should give to the Delawares.

On this intelligence they suspended their cruel purpose and began to collect as many of the prisoners as they had power to deliver; but hearing immediately afterwards that one of our soldiers had been killed near the camp at Muskingum, and that some of their nation were suspected as guilty of the murder, they again imagined they would fall under our resentment, and therefore determined once more to stand out against us. For which purpose, after having brought their prisoners as far as Wakautamike, where they heard this news, they collected them all into a field and were going to kill them, when a second express providentially arrived from Colonel Bouquet, who assured them that their nation was not even suspected of having any concern in the aforesaid murder; upon which they proceeded to the camp to deliver up the captives, who had thus twice so narrowly escaped becoming the victims of their barbarity.

On Friday, November 9th, the colonel, attended by most of the principal officers, went to the conference-house. The Senecas and Delawares were first treated with. Kiyashuta and ten warriors represented the former. Custaloga and twenty warriors the latter.

Kiyashuta spoke—

> With this string of *wampum*, we wipe the tears from your eyes—deliver you these three prisoners, which are the last of your flesh and blood, that remained among the Senecas and Custaloga's tribe of Delawares, we gather together and bury with this belt all the bones of the people that have been killed during this unhappy war, which the Evil Spirit occasioned among us. (A belt or string is always delivered when thus mentioned.) We cover the bones that have been buried, that they may never more be remembered— We again cover their place with leaves that it may be no more—As we have been long astray, and the path between you and us stopped, we extend this belt that it may be again cleared, and we may travel in peace to see our brethren as our ancestors formerly did. While you hold it fast by one end, and we by the other, we shall always be able to discover anything that may disturb our friendship.

The colonel answered that:

He had heard them with pleasure; that he received these three last prisoners they had to deliver and joined in burying the bones of those who had fallen in the war, so that their place might be no more known. The peace you ask for, you shall now have. The king, my master and your father, has appointed me only to make war; but he has other servants who are employed in the work of peace. Sir William Johnson is empowered for that purpose. To him you are to apply; but before I give you leave to go, two things are settled.

1. As peace cannot be finally concluded here, you will deliver me two hostages for the Senecas, and two for Custaloga's tribe, to remain in our hands at Fort Pitt, as a security, that you shall commit no further hostilities or violence against any of His Majesty's subjects; and when the peace is concluded these hostages shall be delivered, safe back to you.

2. The deputies you are to send to Sir William Johnson, must be fully empowered to treat for your tribes, and you shall engage to abide by whatever they stipulate. In that treaty, everything concerning trade and other matters will be settled by Sir William, to render the peace everlasting; and the deputies you are to send to him, as well as the hostages to be delivered to me, are to be named and presented to me for my approbation.

The colonel, after promising to deliver back two of their people, Captain Pipe, and Captain John, whom he had detained at Fort Pitt, took the chiefs by the hand for the first time, which gave them great joy.

The next conference was on November 10th, with the Turky and Turtle tribes of Delawares, King Beaver their chief and thirty warriors representing the former; and Kelappama brother to their chief, (the chief of the Turtle tribe, for some reason, chose to absent himself), with twenty-five warriors the latter. The Seneca's and Custaloga's tribes of Delawares were also present. Their speech and the answer given, were much the same as above;

excepting that the colonel insisted on their delivering up an Englishman, who had murdered one of our people on the frontiers and brought the scalp to them; and that they should appoint the same number of deputies and deliver the same number of hostages, for each of their tribes, as had been stipulated for Custaloga's tribe.

*November 11.* King Beaver presented six hostages to remain with Colonel Bouquet, and five deputies to treat with Sir William Johnson, who were approved of. This day he acquainted the chiefs present that he had great reason to be dissatisfied with the conduct of Nettowhatways, the chief of the Turtle tribe who had not appeared, he therefore deposed him; and that tribe were to choose and present another for his approbation. This they did a few days afterwards—Smile not, reader, at this transaction; for though it may not be attended with so many splendid and flattering circumstances to a commander, as the deposing an East Indian Nabob or chief; yet to penetrate into the wildernesses where those stern West Indian Chieftains hold their sway, and to frown them from their throne; though but composed of the unhewn log, will be found to require both, resolution and. firmness; and their submitting to it clearly shews to what degree of humiliation they were reduced.

But to proceed. The Shawanese still remained to be treated with, and though this nation saw themselves under the necessity of yielding to the same conditions with the other tribes, yet there had appeared a dilatoriness and sullen haughtiness in all their conduct, which rendered it very suspicious.

The 12th of November was appointed for the conference with them; which was managed on their part by Keissinautchtha and Nimwha their chiefs, with the Red Hawke, Lavissimo, Bensivasica, Eweecunwee, Keigleighque, and forty warriors; the Caughnawaga, Seneca and Delaware chiefs, with about sixty warriors, being also present.

The Red Hawke was their speaker, and as he delivered himself with a strange mixture of fierce pride, and humble submission, I shall add a passage or two from his speech.

Brother,

You will listen to us your younger brothers; and as we discover something in your eyes that looks dissatisfaction with us, we now wipe away everything bad between us that you may clearly see—You have heard many bad stories of us—We clean your ears that you may hear—We remove everything bad from your heart, that it may be like the heart of your ancestors, when they thought of nothing but good.

(Here he gave a string.)

Brother; when we saw you coming this road, you advanced towards us with a tomahawk in your hand; but we your younger brothers take it out of your hands and throw it up to God to dispose of as he pleases; by which means we hope never to see it more. (Their usual figure for making peace is burying the hatchet; but as such hatchets may be dug up again, perhaps he thought this new expression of "sending it up to God, or the Good Spirit," a much stronger emblem of the permanency and steadfastness of the peace now to be made.) And now, brother, we beg leave that you who are a warrior, will take hold of this chain (giving a string) of friendship, and receive it from us, who are also warriors, and let us think no more of war, in pity to our old men, women and children. (Intimating, by this last expression, that it was mere compassion to them, and not inability to fight, that made their nation desire peace.)

He then produced a treaty held with the government of Pennsylvania 1701, and three messages or letters from that government of different dates; and concluded thus:

Now, Brother, I beg we who are warriors may forget our disputes and renew the friendship which appears by these papers to have subsisted between our fathers.

He promised, in behalf of the rest of their nation, who were gone to a great distance to hunt, and could not have notice to attend the treaty, that they should certainly come to Fort Pitt in the spring and bring the remainder of the prisoners with them. As the season was far advanced, and the colonel could not stay long in these remote parts, he was obliged to rest satisfied with the prisoners the Shawanese had brought; taking hostages, and laying them under the strongest obligations, for the delivery of the rest; knowing that no other effectual method could at present be pursued.

He expostulated with them on account of their past conduct and told them that the speech they had delivered would have been agreeable to him, if their actions had corresponded with their words. He said:

> You have spoken much or peace, but have neglected, to comply with the only condition, upon which you can obtain it. Keissinautchtha, one of your chiefs, met me a month ago at Tuscarawas, and accepted the same terms of peace for your nation, that were prescribed to the Senecas and Delawares; promising in ten days from that time to meet me here with all your prisoners—After waiting for you till now, you are come at last, only with a part of them, and propose putting off the delivery of the rest till the spring—What right have you to expect different terms from those granted to the Delawares, &c. who have given me entire satisfaction by their ready submission to everything required of them?—But I will cut this matter short with you; and before I explain myself further, I insist on your immediate answer to the following questions—
>
> 1st. Will you forthwith collect and deliver up to me prisoners yet in your possession, and the French living among you, with all the Negroes you have taken from us in this or any other war; and that without any exception or evasion whatsoever?
>
> 2nd. Will you deliver six hostages into my hands as a security for your punctual performance of the above article, and that your nations shall commit no farther hostilities

against the persons or property of His Majesty's subjects?

Benevissico replied that they agreed to give the hostages required and said that he himself would immediately return to their lower towns and collect all our flesh and blood that remained among them, and that we should see them at Fort Pitt as soon as possible. (It will appear, by the postscript to this account, that the Shawanese have fulfilled this engagement.) That, as to the French, they had no power over them. they were subjects to the king of England. We might do with them what we pleased; though he believed they were all returned before this time to their own country.

They then delivered their hostages, and the colonel told them that though he had brought a tomahawk in his hand, yet as they had now submitted, he would not let it fall on their heads, but let it drop to the ground, no more to be seen. He exhorted them to exercise kindness to the captives and look upon them now as brothers and no longer prisoners; adding, that he intended to send some of their relations along with the Indians, to see their friends collected and brought to Fort Pitt. He promised to give them letters to Sir William Johnson, to facilitate a final peace, and desired them to be strong in performing everything stipulated.

The Caughnawagas, the Delawares and Senecas, severally addressed the Shawanese, as grandchildren and nephews, "to perform their promises, and to be strong in doing good, that this peace might be everlasting."

And here I am to enter on a scene, reserved on purpose for this place, that the thread of the foregoing narrative might not be interrupted—a scene, which language indeed can but weakly describe; and to which the poet or painter might have repaired to enrich their highest colourings of the variety of human passions; the philosopher to find ample subject for his most serious reflections; and the man to exercise all the tender and sympathetic feelings of the soul.

The scene I mean, was the arrival of the prisoners in the camp; where were to be seen fathers and mothers recognizing and clasping their once-lost babes; husbands hanging around the necks of their newly-recovered wives; sisters and brothers unexpectedly meeting together after long separation, scarce able to speak the same language, or, for some time, to be sure that they were children of the same parents! In all these interviews, joy and. rapture inexpressible were seen, while feelings of a very different nature were painted in the looks of others;—flying from place to place in eager enquiries after relatives not found! trembling to receive an answer to their questions! distracted with doubts, hopes and fears, on obtaining no account of those they sought for! or stiffened into living monuments of horror and woe, on learning their unhappy fate!

The Indians too, as if wholly forgetting their usual savageness, bore a capital part in heightening this most affecting scene. They delivered up their beloved captives with the utmost reluctance; shed torrents of tears over them, recommending them to the care and protection of the commanding officer. Their regard to them continued all the time they remained in amp. They visited them from day to day; and brought them what corn, skins, horses and other matters, they had bestowed on them, while in their families; accompanied with other presents, and all the marks of the most sincere and tender affection.

Nay, they did not stop here, but, when the army marched, some of the Indians solicited and obtained leave to accompany their former captives all the way to Fort Pitt and employed themselves in hunting and bringing provisions for them on the road. A young Mingo carried this still further and gave an instance of love which would make a figure even in romance. A young woman of Virginia was among the captives, to whom he had formed so strong an attachment, as to call her his wife. Against all remonstrances of the imminent danger to which he exposed himself by approaching to the frontiers, he persisted in following her, at the risk of being killed by the surviving relations of many unfortunate persons, who had been captivated or scalped by those of his nation.

Those qualities in savages challenge our just esteem. They should make us charitably consider their barbarities as the effects of wrong education, and false notions of bravery and heroism; while we should look on their virtues as sure marks that nature has made them fit subjects of cultivation as well as us; and that we are called by our superior advantages to yield them all the helps we can in this way. Cruel and unmerciful as they are, by habit and long example, in war, yet whenever they come to give way to the native dictates of humanity, they exercise virtues which Christians need not blush to imitate.

When they once determine to give life, they give everything with it, which, in their apprehension, belongs to it. From every enquiry that has been made, it appears—that no woman thus saved is preserved from base motives or need fear the violation of her honour. No child is otherwise treated by the persons adopting it than the children of their own body. The perpetual slavery of those captivated in war, is a notion which even their barbarity has not yet suggested to them. Every captive whom their affection, their caprice, or whatever else, leads them to save, is soon incorporated with them, and fares alike with themselves.

These instances of Indian tenderness and humanity were thought worthy of particular notice. The like instances among our own people will not seem strange; and therefore, I shall only mention one, out of a multitude that might be given on this occasion.

Among the captives, a woman was brought into the camp at Muskingum, with a babe about three months old at her breast. One of the Virginia volunteers soon knew her to be his wife, who had been taken by the Indians about six months before. She was immediately delivered to her overjoyed husband. He flew with her to his tent, and cloathed her and his child in proper apparel. But their joy, after the first transports, was soon damped by the reflection that another dear child of about two years old, captivated with the mother, and separated from her, was still missing, although many children had been brought in.

A few days afterwards, a number of other prisoners were brought to the camp, among whom were several more children. The woman was sent for, and one, supposed to be hers, was produced to her. At first sight she was uncertain, but viewing the child with great earnestness, she soon recollected its features;

and was so overcome with joy, that literally forgetting her sucking child she dropt it from her arms and catching up the new-found child in an ecstasy, pressed, it to her breast, and bursting into tears carried it off, unable to speak for joy. The father seizing up the babe she had let fall, followed her in no less transport and affection.

Among the children who had been carried off young, and had long lived with the Indians, it is not to be expected that any marks of joy would appear on being restored to their parents or relatives. Having been accustomed to look upon the Indians as the only connexions they had, having been tenderly treated by them, and speaking their language, it is no wonder that they considered their new state in the light of a captivity, and parted from the savages with tears.

But it must not be denied that there were even some grown persons who shewed an unwillingness to return. The Shawanese were obliged to bind several of their prisoners and force them along to the camp; and some women, who had been delivered up, afterwards found means to escape and run back to the Indian towns. Some, who could not make their escape, clung to their savage acquaintance at parting, and continued many days in bitter lamentations, even refusing sustenance.

For the honour of humanity, we would suppose those persons to have been of the lowest rank, either bred up in ignorance and distressing penury, or who had lived so long with the Indians as to forget all their former connections. For, easy and unconstrained as the savage life is, certainly it could never be put in competition with the blessings of improved life and the light of religion, by any persons who have had the happiness of enjoying, and the capacity of discerning, them.

Everything being now settled with the Indians, the army decamped on Sunday 10th November, and marched for Fort Pitt, where it arrived on the 28th. The regular troops were immediately sent to garrison the different posts on the communication, and the provincial troop., with the captives, to their several provinces. Here ended this expedition, in which it is remarkable that, notwithstanding the many difficulties attending it, the troops were never in warn of any necessaries; continuing perfectly healthy during the whole campaign; in which no life was lost, except the man mentioned to have been killed at Muskingum.

In the beginning of January 1765, Colonel Bouquet arrived at Philadelphia, receiving, wherever he came, every possible mark of gratitude and esteem from the people in general; and particularly from the overjoyed relations of the captives, whom he had so happily, and without bloodshed, restored to their country and friends. Nor was the legislative part of the provinces less sensible of his important services. The assembly of Pennsylvania, at their first sitting, unanimously voted him the following address.

> In Assembly, January 15, 1765, a. m.
> To the Honourable Henry Bouquet, Esq;
> Commander in Chief of his Majesty's Forces in the Southern Department of America,
> The Address of the Representatives of the Freemen of the Province of Pennsylvania, in General Assembly met.
> Sir,
> The representatives of the freemen of the province of Pennsylvania, in general assembly met, being informed that you intend shortly to embark for England, and moved with a due sense of the important services you have rendered to his majesty, his northern colonies in general, and to this province in particular, during our late wars with the French and barbarous Indians, in the remarkable victory over the savage enemy, united to oppose you, near Bushy Run, in August 1763, when on your march for the relief of Pittsburg, owing, under God, to your intrepidity and superior skill in command, together with the bravery of your officers and little army; as also in your late march to the country of the savage nations, with the troops under your direction, thereby striking terror through the numerous Indian tribes around you; laying a foundation for a lasting as well as honourable peace with them; and rescuing, from savage captivity, upwards of two hundred of our Christian brethren, prisoners among them: these

eminent services, and your constant attention to the civil rights of His Majesty's subjects in this province, demand, Sir, the grateful tribute of thanks from all good men; and therefore we, the representatives of the freemen of Pennsylvania, unanimously for ourselves, and in behalf of all the people of this province, do return you our most sincere and hearty thanks for these your great services, wishing you a safe and pleasant voyage to England, with a kind and gracious reception from His Majesty.

Signed, by order of the House,

Joseph Fox, Speaker.

The colonel's answer was as follows, *viz*.

To the Honourable the Representatives of the Freemen of the province of Pennsylvania, in General Assembly met.
Gentlemen,
With a heart impressed with the most lively sense of gratitude, I return you my humble and sincere thanks, for the honour you have done me in your polite address of the 15th of January, transmitted me to New York by your speaker.
Next to the approbation of His Sacred Majesty, and my superior officers, nothing could afford me higher pleasure than your favourable opinion of my conduct, in the discharge of those military commands with which I have been entrusted.
Gratitude as well as justice demand of me to acknowledge, that the aids granted by the legislature of this province, and the constant assistance and. support afforded me by the honourable the Governor and Commissioners in the late expedition, have enabled me to recover so many of His Majesty's subjects from a cruel captivity, and be the happy instrument of restoring them to freedom and liberty: To you therefore, gentlemen, is the greater share of that merit due, which you are generously pleased on this occasion to impute to my services.

Your kind testimony of my constant attention to the civil rights of His Majesty's subjects in this Province, does me singular honour, and calls for the return of my warmest acknowledgements.

Permit me to take this public opportunity of doing justice to the officers of the regular and provincial troops, and the volunteers, who have served with me, by declaring that, under Divine Providence, the repeated successes of His Majesty's arms against a savage enemy, are principally to be ascribed to their courage and resolution, and to their perseverance under the severest hardships and fatigue.

I sincerely wish prosperity and happiness to the province, and have the honour to be, with the greatest respect, Gentlemen,

Your most obedient, and most humble servant,

Henry Bouquet.

Soon afterwards the colonel received a very polite and affectionate letter from Governor Fauquier, dated 25th of December, enclosing resolves of the honourable members of His Majesty's Council, and of the house of Burgesses for the colony and dominion of Virginia.

Those respectable bodies unanimously returned their thanks to him for the activity, spirit and zeal, with which he had reduced the Indians to terms of peace, and compelled those savages to deliver up so many of His Majesty's subjects whom they had in captivity. They further requested the Governor to recommend him to His Majesty's ministers, as an officer of distinguished merit, in this and every former service in which he has been engaged.

The colonel, in his answer, acknowledged the ready assistance and countenance which he had always received from the Governor and colony of Virginia in carrying on the King's service; and mentioned his particular obligations to Colonel Lewis, for his zeal and good conduct during the campaign.

The honours thus bestowed on him, his own modesty made him desirous of transferring to the officers and army under his command; and indeed, the mutual confidence and harmony subsisting between him and them, highly redound to the reputation of both. He has taken every occasion of doing justice to the particular merit of Colonel Reid who was second in command; and also, to all the officers who served in the expedition, regulars as well as provincials. (The Pennsylvania troops were commanded by Lieutenant Colonel Francis, and Lieutenant Colonel Clayton.)

The reader will observe that the public bodies who presented these addresses to the colonel, not only wished to express their own gratitude, but likewise to be instrumental in recommending him to the advancement his services merited. And surely it is a happy circumstance to obtain promotion, not only unenvied, but even with the general approbation and good, wishes, of the public.

It ought, however, to be mentioned, that on the first account His Majesty received of this expedition, and long before those testimonies could reach England, he was graciously pleased of his own royal goodness and as a reward of the colonel's merit, to promote him to the rank of brigadier general, and to the command of the southern district of America. And as he is rendered as dear, by his private virtues, to those who have the honour of his more intimate acquaintance, as he is by his military services to the public, it is hoped he may long continue among us; where his experienced abilities will enable him, and his love of the English constitution entitle him, to fill any future trust to which His Majesty may be pleased to call him.

# Postscript

It was mentioned earlier in this account, that the Shawanese brought only a part of their prisoners with them to Colonel Bouquet at Muskingum, in November last; and that, as the season was far advanced, he was obliged to rest satisfied with taking hostages for the delivery of the remainder at Fort Pitt, in the ensuing spring.

The escape of those hostages soon afterwards, as well as the former equivocal conduct of their nation, had given reason to doubt the sincerity of their intentions with respect to the performance of their promises. But we have the satisfaction to find, that they punctually have fulfilled them.

Ten of their chiefs, and about fifty of their warriors, attended with many of their women and children, met George Croghan, Esq; deputy agent to Sir William Johnson, at Fort Pitt, the 9th of last May; together with a large body of Delawares, Senecas, Sandusky and Munsy Indians; where they delivered the remainder of their prisoners, brightened the chain of friendship, and gave every assurance of their firm intentions to preserve the peace inviolable forever.

There is something remarkable in the appellation they gave to the English on this occasion; calling them Fathers instead of Brethren. Lawaughqua, the Shawanese speaker, delivered. himself in the following terms:

> Fathers, for so we will call you henceforward; listen to what we are going to say to you.
>
> It gave us great pleasure yesterday to be called the children

of the great King of England; and convinces us your intentions towards us are upright, as we know a Father will be tender of his children, and they are more ready to obey him than a Brother. Therefore we hope our Father will now take better care of his children, than has heretofore been done.—

You put us in mind of our promise to Colonel Bouquet; which was to bring your flesh and blood to be delivered at this place. Father, you have not spoke in vain—you see we have brought them with us,—except a few that were out with our hunting parties, which will be brought here as soon as they return.

They have been all united to us by adoption; and although we now deliver them up to you, we will always look upon them as our relations, whenever the Great Spirit is pleased that we may visit them.

Father, We have taken as much care of them, as if they were our own flesh and blood.

They are now become acquainted with your customs and manners; and therefore, we request you will use them tenderly and kindly, which will induce them to live contentedly with you.

Here is a belt with, the figure of our Father the King of Great Britain at one end, and the chief of our nation at the other. It represents them holding the chain of friendship; and we hope neither side will slip their hands from it, so long as the sun and moon give light.

The reader will further remember that one of the engagements which the different Indian Tribes entered into with Colonel Bouquet, was to send deputies to conclude a peace with Sir William Johnson. This has also been punctually fulfilled; and we are assured that Sir William "has finished his congress greatly to his satisfaction, and even beyond his expectations."

Thus, every good consequence has ensued from this important expedition, which our fondest wishes could have induced us to expect from the known valour and spirit of the able commander who had the conduct of it; and we now have the pleasure once more to behold the temple of Janus shut, in this western world!

# Reflections on the War with the Savages of North America

The long continued, ravages of the Indians on the frontiers of the British colonies in America, and the fatal overthrows which they have sometimes given our best disciplined troops, especially in the beginning of the late war, have rendered them an object of our consideration, even in their military capacity. And as but few officers, who may be employed against them, can have opportunities to observe the true causes of their advantages over European troops in the woods, it is with the utmost pleasure that I now proceed to lay before the public the following valuable papers, which I mentioned (see the introduction), to have been communicated to me by an officer of great abilities and long experience, in our wars with the Indians.

As scarce anything has yet been published on a subject now become of the highest importance to our colonies, these papers will undoubtedly be an acceptable present to the reader, and the remarks contained in them may be more and more improved by the future care and attention of able men, till perhaps a complete system is at length formed for the conduct of this particular species of war. (It will appear by the account of Indian tribes and towns annexed to these papers, that the enemies we have to deal with are neither contemptible in numbers or strength.)

# The Temper and Genius of the Indians

The love of liberty is innate in the savage; and seems the ruling passion of the state of nature. His desires and wants, being few, are easily gratified, and leave him much time to spare, which he would spend in idleness, if hunger did not force him to hunt. That exercise makes him strong, active and bold, raises his courage, and fits him for war, in which he uses the same stratagems and cruelty as against the wild beasts; making no scruple to employ treachery and perfidy to vanquish his enemy.

Jealous of his independency and of his property, he will not suffer the least encroachment on either; and upon the slightest suspicion, fired with resentment, he becomes an implacable enemy, and flies to arms to vindicate his right, or revenge an injury.

The advantages of these savages over civilized nations are both natural and acquired. They are tall and well limbed, remarkable for their activity, and have a piercing eye and quick ear, which are of great service to them in the woods.

Like beasts of prey, they are patient, deceitful, and rendered by habit almost insensible to the common feelings of humanity. Their barbarous custom of scalping their enemies, in the heat of action; the exquisite torments often inflicted by them on those reserved for a more deliberate fate; their general ferocity of manners, and the successes wherewith they have often been Hushed, have conspired to render their name terrible, and sometimes to strike a panic even into our bravest and best disciplined troops.

Their acquired advantages are, that they have been inured

to bear the extremes of heat and cold; and from their infancy, in winter and summer, to plunge themselves in cold streams, and to go almost naked, exposed to the scorching sun or nipping frosts, till they arrive to the state of manhood. Some of them destroy the sensation of the skin by scratching it with the short and sharp teeth of some animal, disposed in the form of a curry-comb, which makes them regardless of briers and thorns in running through thickets. Rivers are no obstacles to them in their wild excursions. They either swim over, or cross them on rafts or canoes, of an easy and ready construction.

In their expeditions they live chiefly by hunting, or on wild fruits and roots, with which the woods supply them almost everywhere.

They can bear hunger and thirst for several days, without slackening, on that account, their perseverance in any proposed, enterprise.

By constant practice in hunting, they learn to shoot with great skill; either with bows, or firearms; and to steal unperceived upon their prey, pursuing the tracts of men and beasts, which would be imperceptible to a European. They can run for a whole day without halting, when flying from an enemy, or when sent on any message. They steer, as if by instinct, through trackless woods, and with astonishing patience can lie whole days motionless in ambush to surprise an enemy, esteeming no labour or perseverance too painful to obtain their ends.

They besmear their bodies with bear's grease, which defends them against rains and damps, as well as against the stings of mosquitoes and gnats. It likewise supples their limbs, and makes them as slippery as the ancient gladiators, who could not be held fast when seized in fight.

Plain food, constant exercise, and living in the open air, preserve them healthy and vigorous.

They are powerfully excited to war by the custom established among them, of paying distinguished honours to warriors.

They fight only when they think to have the advantage, but cannot be forced to it, being sure by their speed to elude the most eager pursuit.

Their dress consists of the skins of some wild beast, or a blanket, a shirt either of linen, or of dressed skins, a breech clout, leggings, reaching halfway up the thigh, and fastened to a belt, with *moccasins* on their feet. They use no ligatures that might obstruct the circulation of their blood, or agility of their limbs. They shave their head, reserving only a small tuft of hair on the top; and slit the outer part of the ears, to which, by weights, they give a circular form, extending it down to their shoulders.

They adorn themselves with ear and nose rings, bracelets of silver and *wampum*, and paint their faces with various colours. When they prepare for an engagement they paint themselves black and fight naked.

Their arms are a fusil, or rifle, a powder horn, a shot pouch, a tomahawk, and a scalping knife hanging to their neck.

When they are in want of firearms, they supply them by a bow, a spear, or a death hammer, which is a short club made of hard wood.

Their usual utensils are a kettle, a spoon, a looking glass, an awl, a steel to strike fire, some paint, a pipe and tobacco-pouch. For want of tobacco, they smoke some particular leaves, or the bark of a willow; which is almost their continual occupation.

Thus, lightly equipped do the savages lie in wait to attack, at some difficult pass, the European soldier, heavily accoutred, harassed by a tedious march, and encumbered with an unwieldy convoy.

Experience has convinced us that it is not our interest to be at war with them; but if, after having tried all means to avoid it, they force us to it, (which in all probability will often happen) we should endeavour to fight them upon more equal terms, and regulate our manoeuvres upon those of the enemy we are to engage, and the nature of the country we are to act in.

It does not appear from our accounts of Indian wars, that the savages were as brave formerly as we have found them of late; which must be imputed to their unexpected successes against our troops on some occasions, particularly in 1755; and from the little resistance they have since met with from defenceless inhabitants.

It is certain that even at this day, they seldom expose their persons to danger, and depend entirely upon their dexterity in concealing themselves during an engagement, never appearing openly, unless they have struck their enemies with terror, and have thereby rendered them incapable of defence.—From whence it may be inferred that, if they were beat two or three times, they would lose that confidence inspired by success, and be less inclined to engage in wars which might end fatally for them. But this cannot reasonably be expected, till we have troops trained to fight them in their own way, with the additional advantage of European courage and discipline.

Any deviation from our established military system would be needless, if valour, zeal, order and good conduct, were sufficient to subdue this light-footed enemy. These qualities are conspicuous in our troops; but they are too heavy and indeed too valuable, to be employed alone in a destructive service for which they were never intended. They require the assistance of lighter corps, whose dress, arms and exercises, should be adapted to this new kind of war.

This opinion is supported by the example of many warlike nations, of which I beg leave to mention the following.

The learned Jesuit who has obliged the world with a treatise on the military affairs of the ancient Romans, tells us, from Sallust, that this wise nation, our masters in the art of war,. were never hindered even by the pride of empire, from imitating any foreign maxim or institution, provided it was good; and that they carefully adopted into their own practice whatever they found useful in that of their allies or enemies; so that by receiving some things from one, and some from another, they greatly improved a system even originally excellent.

The defeat of Antony and Crassus by the Parthians, of Curio by the Numidians, and many other instances, convinced the Romans that their legions, who had conquered so many nations, were not fit to engage light-troops, which, harassing them continually, evaded all their endeavours to bring them to a close engagement; and it is probable that if Julius Caesar had not been assassinated, when he was preparing to march against the same

Parthians, to wipe off the reproach of the former defeats, he would have added to his legions a great number of light troops, formed upon the principles and method of that nation, and have left us useful lessons for the conduct of a war against our savages.

That he did not think the attack of irregular troops contemptible, appears clearly in several parts of his commentaries, and particularly in the African war. The various embarrassments he met with from the enemy he had then to deal with, necessarily call to our mind many similar circumstances in the course of our wars with the Indians; and the pains he took to instruct his soldiers to stand and repel the skirmishes of the nimble Africans, may furnish instruction to us in our military operations against the savage Americans.

We are told that:

> While Caesar was on his march to Scipio's quarters, the enemy's horse and light-armed infantry, raising all at once from an ambuscade, appeared upon the hills, and attacked his rear. His legions forming themselves, soon beat the enemy from the higher ground. And now thinking all safe, he begins to pursue his march. But immediately the enemy break forth from the neighbouring hills; and the Numidians, with their light-armed foot, who are wonderfully nimble, always mixing and keeping equal pace with the cavalry in charging or retiring, fall afresh on the Roman foot, thus they frequently renewed the charge, and still retired when he endeavoured to bring them to close engagement. If but two or three of his veterans faced about and cast their piles with vigour, two thousand of the enemy would fly, then returning rally again, making it their business to harass his march, and to press upon his rear, following at some distance and throwing their darts at the legions.

Caesar, having so subtle an enemy to deal with, instructed his soldiers, not like a general who had been victorious in the most arduous exploits, but as a fencing-master, (*lanista*, in Latin, is an instructor of gladiators, which in English can only be translated a fencing-master), would instruct his scholars; teaching them with what pace to retreat from the enemy, and how to return to the charge; how far to advance, and now far to retire; and likewise, in what place and. manner to cast their piles. For their light-armed infantry gave him the greatest uneasiness, deterring his troopers from meeting them, by killing their horses with their javelins, and wearying his legions by their swiftness. For whenever his heavy-armed foot faced about, and endeavoured to return their charge, they quickly avoided the danger by flight.

But without going back to the ancients, we have seen this maxim adopted in our days. Marshal de Saxe finding the French army harassed by the Hussars and other Austrian light troops, formed also several corps of them of different kinds; and the king of Prussia in his first war introduced them into his army, and has augmented and employed them ever since with success. We have ourselves made use of them in the two last wars in Europe: But the light troops wanted in America must be trained on different principles.

The enemies we have to deal with, are infinitely more active and dangerous than the Hussars and Pandours; or even the Africans above-mentioned. For the American savages, after their rapid incursions, retreat to their towns, at a great distance from our settlements, through thickety woods almost impenetrable to our heavy and unwieldy corps, composed of soldiers loaded with cloaths, baggage and provisions, who, when fatigued by a long march, must be a very unequal match to engage the nimble savage in woods, which are his native element.

Another unavoidable encumbrance, in our expeditions, arises from the provisions and baggage of the army, for which a road must be opened, and bridges thrown over rivers and swamps. This creates great labour, retards and weakens the line of march, and keeps the troops tied to a convoy which they cannot lose sight of, without exposing it to become a prey to a vigilant enemy, continually hovering about to seize every advantage.

A European, to be a proper judge of this kind of war, must have lived sometime in the vast forests of America; otherwise he will hardly be able to conceive a continuity of woods without end. In spite of his endeavours, his imagination will betray him into an expectation of open and clear grounds, and he will be apt to calculate his manoeuvres accordingly, too much upon the principle of war in Europe.

Let us suppose a person, who is entirely unacquainted with the nature of this service, to be put at the head of an expedition in America. We will further suppose that he has made the dispositions usual in Europe for a march, or to receive an enemy; and that he is then attacked by the savages. He cannot discover them, though from every tree, log or bush, he receives an incessant fire, and observes that few of their shot are lost. He will not hesitate to charge those invisible enemies, but he will charge in vain. For they are as cautious to avoid a close engagement, as indefatigable in harassing his troops; and notwithstanding all his endeavours, he will still find himself surrounded by a circle of fire, winch, like an artificial horizon, follows him everywhere.

Unable to rid himself of an enemy who never stands his attacks, and flies when pressed, only to return upon him again with equal agility and vigour; he will see the courage of his heavy troops droop, and their strength at last fail them by repeated and ineffectual efforts.

He must therefore think of a retreat, unless he can force his way through the enemy. But how is this to be effected? his baggage and provisions are unloaded and scattered, part of his horses and drivers killed, others dispersed by fear, and his wounded to be carried by soldiers already fainting under the fatigue of a long action. The enemy, encouraged by his distress, will not fail to increase the disorder, by pressing upon him on every side, with redoubled fury and savage howlings.

He will probably form a circle or a square, to keep off so daring an enemy, ready at the least opening to fall upon him with the destructive tomahawk; but these dispositions, though a tolerable shift for defence, are neither proper for an attack, nor a march through the woods.

This is not an imaginary supposition, but the true state of an engagement with the Indians, experienced by the troops who have fought against them. Neither is there anything new or extraordinary in this way of fighting, which seems to have been common to most Barbarians.

What is then to be done to extricate our little army from impending destruction?

This is a problem which I do not pretend to resolve. But as every man would, in similar circumstances, determine himself some way or other, I will propose my own sentiments, founded upon some observations which I believe invariable in all engagements with savages.

The first that their general maxim is to surround their enemy.

The second, that they fight scattered, and never in a compact body.

The third that they never stand their ground when attacked, but immediately give way, to return to the charge.

These principles being admitted, it follows:

1st. That the troops destined to engage Indians, must be lightly cloathed, armed, and accoutred.

2nd. That having no resistance to encounter in the attack or defence, they are not to be drawn up in close order, which would only expose them without necessity to a greater loss.

And, lastly, that all their evolutions must be performed with great rapidity; and the men enabled by exercise to pursue the enemy closely, when put to flight, and not give them time to rally.

These remarks will explain the reasons of the alterations proposed in the formation of a corps of troops, for the service of the woods. It is not, however, to be expected that this method will remove all obstacles, or that those light troops can equal the savages in patience, and activity; but, with discipline and practice, they may in a great measure supply the want of these advantages, and by keeping the enemy at a distance afford great relief and security to the main body.

# General Idea of an Establishment of Light Troops for the Service of the Woods

I shall only venture a few notions suggested by experience upon this subject, chiefly with a view to recommend, it to the consideration of persons capable of proposing a proper method of forming such an establishment: and, in order to be better understood, I will suppose a corps of 500 men to be raised and disciplined for the woods, besides two troops of light horse, to which a company of artificers might be added. The fittest men for that service would be the natives of America bred upon the frontiers, and enlisted between the age of fifteen and twenty years, to be discharged between thirty and thirty-five.

### CLOATHING.

The cloathing of a soldier for the campaign might consist of a short coat of brown cloth, lapelled, and without plaits; a strong tanned shirt, short trowsers, leggings, moccasin or shoe packs, a sailor's hat, a blanket, a knapsack for provisions, and an oiled surtout against the rain. To this might be added, in winter quarters or time of peace, three white shirts and stocks, with a flannel waistcoat.

The surtout watch-coat was contrived by an officer, whose name I do not remember. But instead of the oiled linen to be put under the hat, a cap might perhaps answer better. He writes as follows, *viz.*

As the Indian war will require frequent incursions into a wild country, where a man sick or wounded, is in several respects more detrimental to the service than a man killed, everything that may contribute to the health of the men is of moment.

In this view, I propose a sort of surtout, to preserve men, in a great measure, both from wet and cold.

Take a large checked shirt, of about half a crown sterling per yard, for it should be pretty fine; cut off the wristbands and continue the opening of the breast down to the bottom; sew up the sides from the gussets downwards; rip out the gathers in the fore parts of the collar as far as the shoulder straps, and resew it plain to the collar.

The shirt will then become a sort of watch-coat like a bed-gown, with very wide sleeves.

Take a quantity of linseed oil, and boil it gently till one half is diminished, to which put a small quantity of litharge of gold, and when it is well incorporated with the oil, lay it on with a brush upon the watch-coat, so that it shall be everywhere equally wet.

I suppose the watch-coat, hung in a garret, or other covered place, and so suspended by crooked pins and pack threads in the extremities of the sleeves and edges of the collar, that one part shall not touch another. In a short time, if the weather is good, it will be dry; when a second mixture of the same kind should be laid on with a brush as before. When the second coat of painting is dry, the grease will not come off, and the surtout is an effectual preservative from rain; it is very light to carry, and being pretty full on the back, will not only keep the man dry, but also his pack and ammunition.

The sleeves are left long and wide, to receive the butt end of a firelock (secured) and to cover it below the lock. The coat is double breasted to be lapped over, according to which side. the rain drives. A man will be kept dry by one of these surtouts as far as the knees. If, from the vicinity of the enemy, it is improper to make fires at night, he may place his pack on a stone, and, sitting upon it, change his shoes and leggings, and if he pleases, wrap his blanket round his legs and feet, then drawing the watch-coat close to his body, it will keep him warm, as no air can pass through it, and, leaning against the trunk of a tree, he may pass a tolerable night, both warm and dry.

It would be of service to have a small piece of the same oiled linen to put under the hat or cap to carry the rain down to the watch-coat or surtout, otherwise whatever wet soaks through the hat or cap, will run down the neck, and thereby, in some measure, defeat the design of the watch-coat. Perhaps it might be useful to mix some dark or greenish colour with the oil of the second coating, to make the watch-coat less remarkable in the woods.

## ARMS.

Their arms, the best that could be made, should be short fusils and some rifles, with bayonets in the form of a dirk, to serve for a knife; with powder horns and shot pouches, small hatchets and leathern bottles for water.

## EXERCISES.

The soldiers being raised, cloathed, and formed into companies under proper officers, must, before they are armed, be taught to keep themselves clean, and to dress in a soldier-like manner. This will raise in them a becoming spirit, give them a favourable opinion of their profession, and preserve their health. The first thing they are to learn is to walk well, afterwards to run; and, in order to excite emulation, small premiums might from time to time be given to those who distinguish themselves.

They must then run in ranks, with open files, and wheel in that order, at first slowly, and by degrees increase their speed: this evolution is difficult, but of the utmost consequence to fall unexpectedly upon the flank of the enemy. They are to disperse and rally at given signals; and particular colours should be given to each company, for them to rally by; the men must be used to leap over logs and ditches, and to carry burthens proportioned to then strength.

When the young soldiers are perfect in these exercises, they may receive their arms, with which they are to perform the former evolutions in all sorts of grounds. They will next be taught to handle their arms with dexterity; and, without losing time upon trifles, to load and fire very quick, standing, kneeling, or lying on the ground. They are to fire at a mark without a rest, and not suffered to be too long in taking aim. Hunting and small premiums will soon make them expert marksmen.

They ought to learn to swim, pushing at the same time their cloaths, arms, and ammunition before them, on a small raft; and to make use of snow shoes. They must then be set to work, and be taught to throw up an entrenchment, open a trench, make fascines, clays and gabions; likewise, to fall trees, square logs, saw planks, make canoes, carts, ploughs, hand and wheel barrows, shingles and clap-boards, casks, *bateaus* and bridges, and to build log houses, ovens, &c.

By example and practice, the most ingenious among them will soon become tolerable good carpenters, joiners, wheelwrights, coopers, armourers, smiths, masons, brickmakers, saddlers, tailors, butchers, bakers, shoemakers, couriers, &c.

## LIGHT HORSE AND DOGS.

I said that, to complete this establishment, they should have two troops of light horse, supposed of fifty men each, officers included. The men are to perform the same exercises as the foot, and afterwards be taught to ride, and particularly to be very alert at mounting and dismounting with their arms in their hands, to gallop through the woods, up and down hills, and leap over logs and ditches.

The horses ought to be bought up on the frontiers, where they are bred and used to feed in the woods, and are strong and hardy. They are to be thoroughly broke, made to stand fire, to swim over rivers, &c. their saddles and accoutrements very simple, strong and light. The number of horses might be reduced to one-half, in time of peace, though they would be of little expense, as they might be bred and maintained without charge in the military settlement. This corps should be equipped as the foot, having only a short rifle in lieu of a fusil, and a battle axe with a long handle, the only sort of arms they should make use of in the charge.

Every light horseman ought to be provided with a bloodhound, which would be useful to find out the enemies' ambushes, and to follow their tracts; they would seize the naked savages, or at least give time to the horse men to come up with them; they would add to the safety of the camp at night by discovering any attempt to surprise it.

## ARTIFICERS.

The company of artificers should be composed of the most useful tradesmen, and ought to be maintained at all times for the instruction of the soldiers, the use of the settlement, or the service of the army, during the campaign. It will now be time to draw forth this military colony and remove them to the ground laid out for that use in the woods, and at a good distance from the inhabitants. The nature of this settlement will hereafter be more particularly described.

Necessity creating industry, our young soldiers will soon provide themselves with the most useful articles, and in a couple of years be able to raise provisions for themselves.

While the greatest part would be employed in clearing the ground, fencing, ploughing, sowing, planting, building and making utensils and household furniture, others might hunt with their officers, and remain a fortnight or a month out of the camp, without other provisions than a little flour, and what they could procure by hunting and fishing: then to be relieved, and the whole trained up in that way.

The military exercises must still be kept up and practised, and great care taken to inculcate and preserve purity of manners, obedience, order and decency among the men, which will be found much easier in the woods than in the neighbourhood of towns.

In order to make this military establishment more generally

useful; I would propose that the soldiers should only receive a very small part of their pay; leaving the remainder in the military chest.

Their accounts should be settled every year, and when their services should in title them to their discharge, I could wish that each of them had 200 acres of land given him, in a district appropriated for that purpose; and receiving then the whole balance of pay due them, they would then be enabled to complete their settlement. This institution appears not only practicable, but easy, if attended to with patience, assiduity and firmness. The plan I would propose is as follows.

Method of forming such settlements upon the frontiers, as might support themselves during an Indian War.

Let us suppose a settlement to be formed for one hundred families, composed of five persons each, upon an average.

Lay out upon a river or creek, if it can be found conveniently, a square of one thousand seven hundred and sixty yards, or a mile for each side.

That square will contain as follows 640 acres:
Allowing for streets and public uses 40
To half an acre for every house 50
To one hundred lots at five and half acres 550

The four sides of the square measure 7040 yards, which gives to each house about seventy yards front to stockade, and the ground allowed for building will be 210 feet front, and about 100 feet deep.

An acre of ground will produce at least thirty bushels of Indian corn. Therefore, two acres are sufficient to supply five persons, at the rate of twelve bushels each person. Two other acres will be a pasture for cows and sheep, another acre for hay, to be sown with red clover. The remaining half acre may be laid out for a garden.

Round the town are the commons, of three miles square, containing, exclusive of the lots above-mentioned, 5120 acres. On three sides of the town, five other squares will be laid out of three square miles, containing 5760 acres each, one of which is reserved for wood for the use of the settlement; the other four

## THE FOLLOWING IS A ROUGH SKETCH OF THE WHOLE.

| Township A. | | | Township B. | | | Township C. | | | Township D. | |
|---|---|---|---|---|---|---|---|---|---|---|
| 1 | 1 | Commons / A / Commons | 2 | Commons / B / Commons | Wood for the Town B | 3 | Wood for the Town C | Commons / C / Commons | 4 | Commons / D / Commons | Wood for the Town D | 4 |
| 5260 acres wood for the Town A | | | | | | | | | | |
| 25 lotts of 250 acres 1 | 1 | | 2 | | | 3 | | | 4 | |

to be divided into 25 out-lots or plantations, of about 230 acres each, so that in the four squares, there will be one hundred such plantations, for the 100 families.

Another township may be laid out joining this, upon the same plan, and as many more as you please upon the same line, without losing any ground.

Thus the town, A, has its commons, its woodland, and its four squares marked No. 1. each containing twenty-five plantations of 230 acres, as proposed above. In like manner, the other towns, B, C, D, have their appurtenances respectively marked.

Let us now suppose this plan accomplished, and such corps as these fully settled, trained and disciplined, in the manner above-mentioned; I would ask whether any officer, entrusted with an expedition against the savages, would not chose to have them in his army? I may safely answer for all those who have been employed in that service, that they would prefer them to double the number of the best European troops.

And when they had served the time limited, namely from their 15th to their 35th year, what vast satisfaction would it be to pay over to them their share of savings from the public chest; and, as a reward of their faithful toils, to vest them and their heirs with their several plantations, which they would now be enabled to cultivate as their own? This prospect would engage many people to enter their sons, in such corps; and those veterans, when thus discharged, would not only be the means of forming and animating others by their example, but in case of a war would still bravely maintain the property they had so honourably acquired, and be the greatest security of the frontier where they are settled.

## PREPARATIONS FOR AN EXPEDITION IN THE WOODS AGAINST SAVAGES.

It is not practicable to employ large bodies of troops against Indians; the convoys necessary for their support would be too cumbersome, and could neither be moved with ease, nor protected. It would be better to fit out several small expeditions, than one too unwieldy: I will therefore suppose that a corps intended to act offensively shall not exceed the following proportions.

|  |  |
|---|---|
| Two regiments of foot | 900 |
| One battalion of hunters | 500 |
| Two troops of light horse | 100 |
| One company of artificers | 20 |
| Drivers and necessary followers | 280 |
| In all | 1800 |

The first article to provide is the provision, and next the carriages.

The daily ration of a soldier in the woods should consist of one pound and a half of meat (which requires no carriage) and. one pound, of flour, with a gill of salt per week.

|  |  |
|---|---|
| Upon that allowance 1800 men will require for six months or 182 days | 327,600 lb. Flour. |
| Allowing one fourth, for accident | 81,900 |
| For six months | 409,500 lb. Flour. |
| Meat for the same time with a fourth part more for accidents, or 2048 beeves at 300 lb. each | 614,400 lb. Meat. |
| Salt for 26 weeks | 182 Bushels; |

The above quantity would serve the whole campaign, but one half would be sufficient to penetrate from the last deposit into the heart of the enemy's country: therefore, we shall compute the carriages for this last quantity only.

Every horse carries about 150 lb. neat weight, therefore, to carry flour for three months or 204,750 lb. will require 1365 horses.

|  |  |
|---|---|
| Horses for flour brought forward | 365 |
| For 91 Bushels of salt | 46 |
| Ammunition | 50 |
| Tents | 50 |
| Tools | 50 |
| Hospital | 20 |
| Officer's baggage and staff | 50 |
|  | 1731 |

To reduce this exorbitant number of horses, and the great expense attending it, I would propose, for such parts of the country as would admit of it, to make use of carts, drawn each by four oxen, and carrying about 1300 lb. or six barrels of flour.

The above quantity of 204,750 lb. will then be carried by
160 carts drawn by                    640 oxen
Spare oxen with the army     384
The number of oxen wanted  1024

This method would not be as expeditious as the carriage by horses, and would require more time and. attention in cutting the road, and bridging the swampy places, &c. but, on the other hand, what an expense would be saved! and by killing the oxen in proportion as the flour is used, and abandoning the carts, the convoy is daily reduced, and the grass near the encampment will not be so soon consumed, which is not the case with horses, which must equally be fed though unloaded. This is an object of consequence, particularly near the end of the campaign, when the scarcity of fodder obliges to move the camps every day, and to place them in low and disadvantageous grounds.

It would therefore incline for the use of carts, and they could be made before hand by the hunters and their artificers.

The oxen should be brought in the provinces where the farmers make use of them in their works. One or two soldiers would drive the cart and take charge of the four oxen.

There are few rivers in North-America deep in summer, and which these carts with high and broad wheels, could not ford; but if the contrary should happen, the carts, provisions and baggage, may be rafted over, or a bridge built. In a country full of timber, and with troops accustomed to work, no river will stop an army for a long time.

By the above method, 300 or 400 horses would be sufficient to carry the baggage, ammunition, tents, tools, &c.

EXPLANATION OF THE FOUR PLANS FOLLOWING

Representing the different positions of our army in the woods.

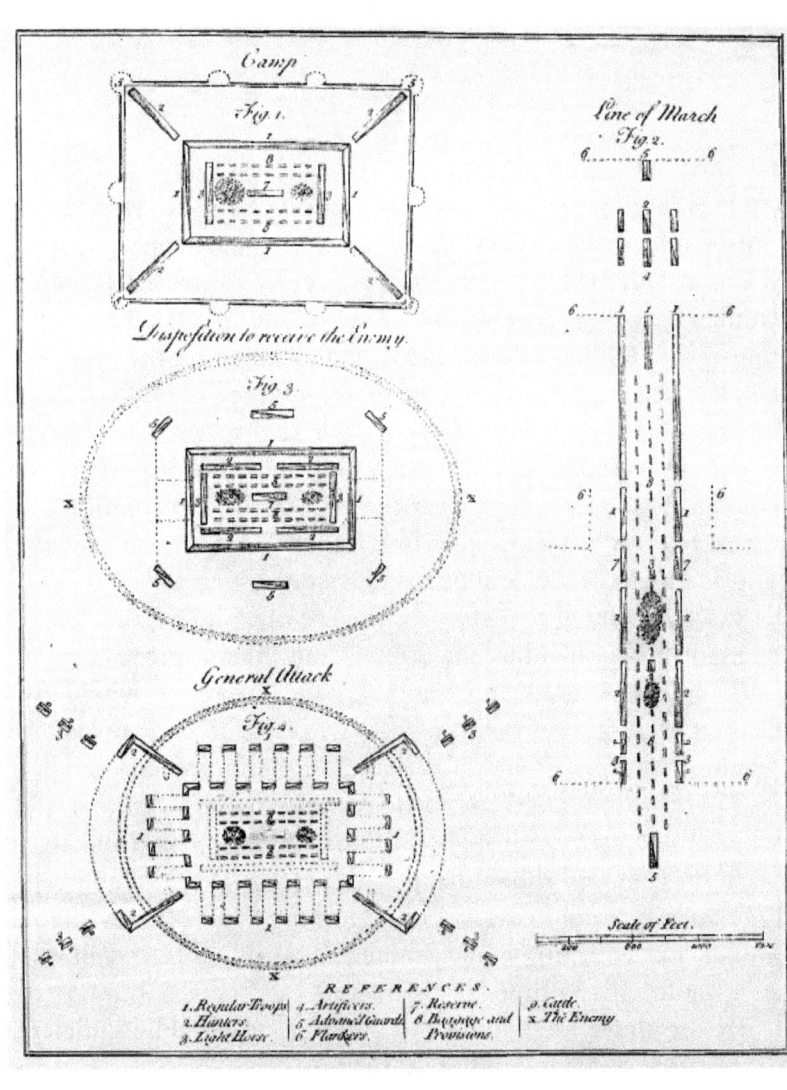

## ENCAMPMENT.

The camp (fig. 1) forms a parallelogram, of one thousand by six hundred feet. Eight hundred men of the regular troops (1) encamp on the four sides, which gives twenty-four feet to each tent, containing six men. The light horse (3) encamp within the parallelogram. The reserve (7) in the centre.

The provisions, ammunition, tools, and stores (8) and the cattle (9) are placed between the two troops of light horse and the reserve. The hunters (2) encamp on the outside diagonally at the four angles, being covered by redoubts (5) formed with kegs and bags of flour or fascines. Besides these four redoubts, another is placed to the front, one to the rear, and two before each of the long faces of the camp, making in all ten advanced guards of twenty-two men each, and seven sentries, covered if possible by breast works of fascines or provisions.

Before the army lay down their arms, the ground is to be reconnoitred, and the guards posted, who will immediately open a communication from one to the other to relieve the sentries and facilitate the passage of rounds.

The sentries upon the ammunition, provisions, headquarters, and. all others in the inside of the camp are furnished from the reserve. The officers, except the staff and commanders of corps, encamp on the line with their men.

The fires are made between the guards and camp and put out in case of an attack in the night.

## LINE OF MARCH. FIG. 2

Part of the hunters (2) in three divisions detaching small parties (5, 6) to their front and to their right and left, to search the woods and discover the enemy.

The artificers and axe-men (4) to cut a road for the convoy, and two paths on the right and left for the troops.

One hundred and fifty of the regular troops (1) in two files, who are to form the front of the square; these march in the centre road.

Two hundred and fifty regulars (1) in one file by the right-hand path; and 250 (1) by the left-hand path, are to form the long faces.

These are followed by 150 regulars (1) in two files, who are to form the rear of the square.

The reserve (7) composed of 100 regulars in two files. The rest of the hunters (2) in two files.

The light horse. (3)

The rear-guard (5) composed, of hunters, follows the convoy at some distance and closes the march. The scouting parties (6) who flank the line of march, are taken from the hunters and light horse, and posted as in plan (fig. 2) , some orderly light horse men, attend the general and field officers who command the grand divisions, to carry their orders. Two guards of light horse take charge of the cattle. (8)

The convoy proceeds in the following order.

The tools and ammunition following the front column.

The baggage.

The cattle.

The provisions.

The whole divided into brigades, and the horses two a breast.

## DEFILES.

In case of a defile, the whole halt until the ground is reconnoitred, and the hunters have taken possession of the heights. The centre column then enters into the defile, followed by the right face; after them the convoy; then the left and rear face, with the reserve, the light horse, and the rear guard.

The whole to form again as soon as the ground permits.

## DISPOSITION TO RECEIVE THE ENEMY. (FIG. 3)

The whole halt to form the square or parallelogram, which is done thus. The two first men of the centre column stand fast at two yards distance. The two men following them, step forward and post themselves at two yards on the right and left. The others come to the front in the same manner, till the two files have formed a rank, which is the front of the square.

The rear face is formed by the two file-leaders turning to the centre road, where having placed themselves at two yards distance, they face outwards, and are followed by their files, each man posting himself on their right or left, and facing towards the enemy the moment he comes to his post.

As soon as the front and rear are extended and formed, the two long faces, which have in the meantime faced outwards, join now the extremities of the two fronts and close the square. (These evolutions must be performed with celerity.)

## TO REDUCE THE SQUARE.

The right and left of the front, face to the centre, where the two centre men stand fast. Upon the word "march" these step forward and are replaced by the two next, who follow them, and so on; by which means, that front becomes again a column. The rear goes to the right about, and each of the two centre men leads again to the side paths followed by the rest.

While the troops form, the light horse and each division of the convoy take the ground assigned to them within the square, as if they were to encamp; and the horses being unloaded, two parallel lines will be formed, with the bags and kegs of provisions, to cover the wounded and the men unfit for action. The hunters, take post on the most advantageous ground on the outside, and skirmish with the enemy, till the square is formed; when, upon receiving their orders, they retire within the square, where they take their post as in (Fig. 3).

The small parties of rangers (5) who have flanked the line of march, remain on the outside, to keep off the enemy and observe their motions.

When the firing begins the troops will have orders to fall on their knees, to be less exposed till it is thought proper to attack.

The four faces, formed by the regular troops, are divided into platoons chequered. One half, composed of the best and most active soldiers, is called the First Firing, and the other half the Second Firing.

The eight platoons at the angles are of the second firing, in order to preserve the form of the square during the attack.

It is evident that, by this disposition, the convoy is well covered, and the light troops, destined for the charge, remain concealed; and as all unexpected events during an engagement are apt to strike terror, and create confusion, among the enemy, it is natural to expect that the savages will be greatly disconcerted at the sudden and unforeseen eruption, that will soon pour upon them from the inside of the square; and that, being vigorously attacked in front and flank at the same time, they will neither be able to resist, nor, when once broke, have time to rally, so as to make another stand. This may be effected in the following manner.

## GENERAL ATTACK. FIG. 4

The regulars (1) stand fast.

The hunters (2) sally out, in four columns, through the intervals of the front and rear of the square, followed by the light horse (3) with their bloodhounds. The intervals of the two columns who attack in the front, and of those who attack in the rear, will be closed by the little parties of rangers (5) posted, at the angles of the square, each attack forming in that manner, three sides of a parallelogram. In that order they run to the enemy (X) and having forced their way through their circle, fall upon their flanks; by wheeling to their right and left, and charging with impetuosity.

The moment they take the enemy in flank, the First Firing of the regular troops march out briskly and attack the enemy in front. The platoons detached in that manner from the two short faces, proceed only about one hundred yards to their front, where they halt to cover the square, while the rest of the troops who have attacked pursue the enemy, till they are totally dispersed, not giving them time to recover themselves.

The sick and wounded, unable to march or ride, are transported in litters made of flour bags, through which two long poles are passed, and kept asunder by two sticks, tied across beyond the head and feet to stretch the bag. Each litter is carried by two horses—

These remarks might have been extended to many other cases that may occur in the course of a campaign or of an engagement, but it is hoped this sketch will be sufficient to evince the necessity of some alteration in our ordinary method of proceeding in an Indian war.

# Appendix 1

## CONSTRUCTION OF FORTS AGAINST INDIANS

As we have not to guard here against cannon, the system of European fortifications may be laid, aside, as expensive, and not answering the purpose. Forts against Indians, being commonly remote from our settlements, require a great deal of room to lodge a sufficient quantity of stores and provisions, and at the same time ought to be defensible with one half of their complete garrisons, in case of detachments or convoys.

I am therefore of opinion that a square or pentagon, with a block-house of brick or stone at every angle, joined by a wall flanked by the blockhouses, would be the best defence against such enemies. (Experience has demonstrated that fortifications made of wood decay very soon and are on that account of considerable expense.) A ditch from seven to eight feet deep might be added, with loop holes in the cellars of the block-houses six feet from the ground, to defend the ditch.

Along the inside of the curtains the traders might build houses and stores, covered as well as the block-houses with tiles, or slate, to guard against fire arrows. There will remain a spacious area for free air and use, in which as well as in the ditch, gardens might be made and wells dug.

The powder magazines might be placed in the centre of the area, keeping only a small quantity of cartridges in each block-house for present use.

The garrisons of such forts would be free from surprises, even if they had no sentries, for nothing can get at them, while the doors are well bolted and barred.

## SOME REASONS FOR KEEPING POSSESSION OF OUR LARGE FORTS IN THE INDIAN COUNTRY:

As these forts have been one of the causes of the last war and are a great eyesore to the savages, they have bent their chief efforts against them; and therefore, while thus employed, they have been less able to distress our settlements. Our forts keep the Indian towns at a great distance from us. Fort Pitt has effectually driven them beyond the Ohio and made them remove their settlements at least sixty miles further westward. Was it not for these forts, they would settle close on our borders, and in time of war infest us every day in such numbers as would overpower the thin inhabitants scattered on our extensive frontier.

The farmer unable to sow or reap would soon fall back on our chief towns or quit the country for want of bread. In either case, what would be the fate of the large towns burthened with the whole country, and deprived of subsistence and of the materials of trade and export?

The destruction of these forts being, in time of war, the chief aim of the savages, they gather about them to distress the garrisons, and to attack the convoys; thereby giving us an opportunity to fight them in a body, and to strike a heavy blow, which otherwise they would never put in our power, as their advantage lies in surprises, which are best erected by small numbers. Experience has convinced them that it is not in their power to break those shackles, and therefore it is not probable that they will renew the attempt; and our posts will continue a check upon them and save the difficulty and expense of taking post again in their country.

Our forts are likewise the proper places for trade, which being closely inspected, it will be easy for us to limit their supplies, to such commodities as they cannot turn against us, and to put a speedy stop to all just causes of complaints, by giving immediate redress.

A few forts, with strong garrisons, I should judge to be of more service than a greater number weakly guarded. In the last war we lost all our small posts; but our more considerable ones, Detroit and Fort Pitt, resisted all the efforts of the savages, by the strength of their garrisons.

# Appendix 2

The following paper was written by an officer well acquainted with the places he describes; and is thought worthy of a place here as everything is material which can increase our knowledge of the vast countries ceded to us and of the various nations that inhabit them.

Account of the French Forts Ceded to Great Britain in Louisiana:

The settlement of the Illinois being in 40 degrees of latitude, is 500 leagues from New Orleans by water and 350 by land.

The most proper time of the year for going there, is the beginning of February. The waters of the Mississippi are then high, and the country being overflowed, there is less to fear from the savages, who are hunting in that season.

The encampments should be on the left of the river, as the enemies are on the right, and cannot have a sufficient number of crafts to cross if their party is large. They generally attack at daybreak, or at the time of embarking. The inhabitants might bring provisions halfway, if they were allowed good pay.

The Delawares and Shawanese lie near Fort Duquesne, which is about 500 leagues from the Illinois. The Wiandots and Ottawas, (who are at the Detroit) are about 250 leagues from the Illinois by land. And the Miamis about 200 by land.

✶✶✶✶✶✶

Part of the navigation of the Ohio, from Fort Pitt is described as follows, *viz*. That the difficult part of the river is from Fort Pitt about fifty or sixty miles downwards. There are fifty-two islands between Fort Pitt and the lower Shawanese town on Scioto; and none of them difficult to pass in the night, but one at the mouth of Muskingum, occasioned by a number of trees lying in the channel. From the lower Shawanese Town to the falls, there are but eight or nine islands. At the falls, the river is very broad, with only one passage on the east side, in which there is water enough at all seasons of the year to pass without difficulty. Below the falls, the navigation is every way clear down to the Mississippi.

✶✶✶✶✶✶

Nevertheless, as intelligence is carried very fast by the savages, and as all the nations with whom we are at war, can come by the Ohio, we must be vigilant to prevent a surprise.

The mouth of the Ohio, in the Mississippi, is thirty-five leagues from the Illinois.

Thirteen leagues from the Mississippi, on the left of the Ohio, is Fort Massiac, or Assumption, built in 1757, a little below the mouth of the River Cherokee. (The Cherokee falls into the Ohio about 800 miles below Fort Pitt. This river is in general wide and shoal up to the south mountain, passable only with bark canoes, after which it grows very small.) It is only a stockade, with four bastions and eight pieces of cannon. It may contain 100 men. In four days one may go by land, from this fort to the Illinois.

It is of consequence for the English to preserve it, as it secures the communication between the Illinois and Fort Pitt.

Fort Vincennes, which is the last post belonging to Louisiana, is upon the River Ouabache, sixty leagues from its conflux with the Ohio. (The Ouabache or Wabash empties itself into the Ohio about sixty miles above the Cherokee River, on the opposite or west side.) It is a small stockade fort, in which there may be about twenty soldiers. There are also a few inhabitants. The soil is extremely fertile and produces plenty of corn and tobacco.

The distance from this fort to the Illinois, is 155 leagues by water. And it may be travelled by land in six days.

The nation of savages living at this post is called Pianquicha.

It can furnish sixty warriors.

Although we do not occupy Fort Vincennes at present, yet it would be of the utmost consequence for us to settle it, as there is a communication from it with Canada, by going up the Ouabache.

From this post to the Ouachtanons is sixty leagues, and from thence to the Miamis (still going up the Ouabache) is sixty leagues further; then there is a portage of six leagues to the river Miamis, and you go down that river twenty-four leagues to Lake Erie.

Mr. Daurby went by that route in 1759 from the Illinois to Venango, with above 400 men, and two hundred thousand weight of flour.

★★★★★★

By the above paper the rout is given up the Mississippi, part of the Ohio, and up the Ouabache to Fort Vincennes, and likewise to the Illinois. Again, from Vincennes and the Ouachtanons by water, on the westerly communication to the Miamis portage, then by water down that river by the easterly rout into Lake Erie, proceeding as far as Presqu' Isle, then by the 15 m. portage into Buffalo or Beef River, lately called French Creek, then down the same to Venango on the Ohio. In order, therefore, to carry this rout still further, we shall continue it from Venango to the mouth of Juniata in Susquehannah, which brings it within the settled parts of Pennsylvania, *viz.*

From Venango to Licking Creek, ten miles. To Toby's Creek, thirteen. To a small creek, one. To the parting of the road, five. To a large run, three. To Leycaumeyhoning, nine. To Pine Creek, seven. To Chuckcaughting, eight. To Weeling Creek, four. To the crossing of *ditto*, four. To a miry swamp, eight. To the head of Susquehanna, ten. To Meytauning Creek, eighteen. To Clear Field Creek, six. To the top of Allegheny, one. To the other side *ditto*, six. To Beaver dams, five. To Franks town, five. To the Canoe place, six. To the mouth of Juniata, 110. Total 239 miles.

✶✶✶✶✶✶

Thirty-five leagues from the mouth of the Ohio, in going up the Mississippi, on the right, is the River Kaskasquias. Two leagues up this river, on the left, is the settlement of the Kaskasquias, which is the most considerable of the Illinois.

There is a fort built upon the height on the other side of the river, over against Kaskasquias; which, as the river is narrow, commands and protects the town.

I don't know how many guns there may be, nor how many men it may contain. There may be about 400 inhabitants.

The Illinois Indians, called Kaskasquias, are settled half a league from the town; and are able to turn out 100 warriors. They are very lazy and great drunkards.

Six leagues from Kaskasquias, on the bank of the Mississippi, is Fort Chartres, built of stone, and can contain 300 soldiers. There may be twenty cannon at most, and about 100 inhabitants round. Chartres.

The Illinois Indians at that place, who are called Metchis, can furnish forty warriors.

Between the Kaskasquias, and Fort Chartres, is a small village, called *La prairie due Rocher* (the Rock Meadow) containing about fifty white inhabitants; but there is neither fort nor savages.

Near Fort Chartres is a little village, in which is about a score of inhabitants. Here are neither savages nor fort.

Fifteen leagues from Fort Chartres, going up the Mississippi, is the village of the Casquiars. There is a small stockade fort; I don't know if there is any cannon. There may be about 100 inhabitants.

The Illinois Indians living near this village are called Casquiars and can turn out sixty warriors.

I compute that there are about 300 Negroes at the Illinois.

The country of the Illinois is fertile, producing good wheat and corn. All kinds of European fruits succeed there surprisingly well, and they have wild grapes with which they make tolerable wine. Their beer is pretty good.

There are mines of lead, and some salt. They make sugar of maple, and there are stone quarries.

# Appendix 3

ROUT from PHILADELPHIA to FORT-PITT.

|  | Miles | Qrs. | Per. |
|---|---|---|---|
| From PHILADELPHIA to Lancaster | 66 | 0 | 38 |
| to Carlisle | 55 | 0 | 00 |
| to Shippensburgh | 22 | 0 | 00 |
| to Fort Loudoun | 24 | 2 | 00 |
| to Fort Littleton | 17 | 3 | 00 |
| to the crossing of the Juniata | 18 | 2 | 00 |
| to Fort Bedford | 14 | 2 | 00 |
| to the crossing of Stoney creek | 29 | 0 | 39 |
| to Fort Ligonier | 20 | 1 | 43 |
| to Fort Pitt | 56 | 0 | 00 |
|  | 324 | 2 | 40 |

# Appendix 4

| | Distance from one another. Miles. | Distance from Fort-Pitt. Miles. |
|---|---|---|
| **First ROUT about N. N. W.** | | |
| From Fort Pitt to Kushkuskies Town on Big Beaver-Creek | | 45 |
| up the east branch of Beaver-Creek to Shaningo. | 15 | 60 |
| up ditto to Pematuning.. | 12 | 72 |
| to Mohoning on the West branch of Beaver Creek | 32 | 104 |
| up the branch to Salt Lick | 10 | 114 |
| to Cayahoga River........ | 32 | 146 |
| to Ottawas town on Cayahoga ................ | 10 | 156 |

| | Distance from one another. Miles. | Distance from Fort-Pitt. Miles. |
|---|---|---|
| **Second ROUT W. N. W.** | | |
| From Fort Pitt to the mouth of Big Beaver-Creek ........ | | 25 |
| to Tuscarawas............ | 91 | 116 |
| to Mohickon John's Town | 50 | 166 |
| to Junundat or Wyandot town ................ | 46 | 212 |
| to Sandusky ............ | 4 | 216 |
| to Junqueindundeh ...... | 24 | 240 |

247

### Third ROUT about W. S. W.

| | | |
|---|---:|---:|
| From Fort Pitt to the Forks of the Muskingham ............... | | 128 |
| to Bullet's Town on Muskingham ............... | 6 | 134 |
| to Waukatamike ......... | 10 | 144 |
| to King Beaver's Town on the heads of the Hockhocking ............... | 27 | 171 |
| to the lower Shawanese Town on Sioto River... | 40 | 211 |
| to the Salt Lick town on the heads of Sioto..... | 25 | 236 |
| to the Miamis Fort........ | 190 | 429 |

### Fourth ROUT down the Ohio; general course about S. W.

| | Distance from one another. Miles. | Distance from Fort-Pitt. Miles. |
|---|---:|---:|
| By water from Fort Pitt to the mouth of Big Beaver Creek..... | | 27 |
| to the mouth of Little Beaver Creek ........ | 12 | 39 |
| to the mouth of Yellow Creek ............... | 10 | 49 |
| to the two Creeks........ | 18 | 67 |
| to Weeling ............... | 6 | 73 |
| to Pipe Hill.............. | 12 | 85 |
| to the long Reach........ | 30 | 115 |
| to the foot of the Reach.. | 18 | 133 |
| to the mouth of the Muskingham River ....... | 30 | 163 |
| to the little Canhawa river. | 12 | 175 |
| to the mouth of Hockhocking river ......... | 13 | 188 |
| to the mouth of Letort's creek ................ | 40 | 228 |
| to Kiskeminetas ......... | 33 | 261 |
| to the mouth of big Canhawa or new river..... | 8 | 269 |
| to the mouth of big Sandy creek ................ | 40 | 309 |
| to the mouth of Sioto river | 40 | 349 |
| to the mouth of big Salt Lick river ............ | 30 | 379 |
| to the Island............ | 20 | 399 |

|  | Distance from one another. Miles. | Distance from Fort-Pitt. Miles. |
|---|---|---|
| to the mouth of little Mineamie or Miammeet river | 55 | 454 |
| to big Miammee or Rocky river | 30 | 484 |
| to the Big Bonest | 20 | 504 |
| to Kentucky river | 55 | 559 |
| to the Falls of the Ohio | 50 | 609 |
| to the Wabash, or Ouabache | 131 | 740 |
| to Cherokee River | 60 | 800 |
| to the Mississippi | 40 | 840 |

The rivers, called little and Great Mineamie or Miammee, fall into the Ohio between Sioto and Oubache, and are different from the Miamis River, which runs into the west end of Lake Erie, below the Miamis Fort.

The River Big Bones is so called from elephant's bones said to be found there.

N.B. The places mentioned in the three first routs are delineated in the foregoing map, by an officer who has an actual knowledge of most of them and has long served against the Indians. The fourth rout down the Ohio was given by an Indian trader, who has often passed from Fort Pitt to the Falls; and the distances he gives of the mouths of the several rivers that fall into the Ohio may be pretty certainly depended on.

# Appendix 5

Names of different Indian Nations in North America, with the numbers of their fighting men; referred to in the note earlier.

The following list was drawn up by a French trader, a person of considerable note, who has resided many years among the Indians, and still continues at Detroit, having taken the oaths of allegiance to the King of Great Britain. His account may be depended on, so far as matters of this kind can be brought near the truth; a great part of it being delivered from his own personal knowledge.

|  | Warriors |
|---|---|
| Conawughrunas, near the falls of St. Louis | 200 |
| Abenaquis ⎫ | 350 |
| Michmacs ⎪ | 550 |
| *Amalistes ⎬ St. Lawrence Indians | 700 |
| *Chalas ⎭ | 130 |
| Nipissins ⎫ living towards the heads of the | 400 |
| Algonquins ⎭ Ottawa river | 300 |
| Les Tetes de Boule, or Round Heads, near the above | 2,500 |
| Six Nations, on the frontiers of New York, &c. | 1,550 |
| Wiandots, near lake Erie | 300 |
| Chipwas ⎫ near the Lakes Superior and Michigan | 5,000 |
| Ottawas ⎭ | 900 |
| Messesagues, or River Indians, being wandering tribes, on the lakes Huron and Superior | 2,000 |
| Powtewatamis, near St. Joseph's and Detroit | 350 |
| Les Puans | 700 |
| Folle avoine, or Wild-Oat Indians ⎬ near Puans bay | 350 |
| *Mechecouakis ⎫ | 250 |
| Sakis ⎬ South of Puans bay | 400 |
| Mascoutens ⎭ | 500 |

|  | Warriors |
|---|---|
| Ouisconsins, on a river of that name, falling into the Mississippi on the east side | 550 |
| Christinaux | 3,000 |
| Assinaboes, or Assinipouals .. } of the same name | 1,500 |
| Blancs†Barbus, or White Indians with Beards | 1,500 |
| Sioux, of the meadows. } towards the heads of | 2,500 |
| Sioux, of the woods .... } Mississippi | 1,800 |
| Missouri, on the river of that name | 3,000 |
| *Grandes Eaux | 1,000 |
| Osages | 600 |
| Canses | 1,600 |
| Panis blancs ..... } south of Missouri | 2,000 |
| Panis piques | 1,700 |
| Padoucas | 500 |
| Ajoues, north of the same | 1,100 |
| Arkanses, on the river that bears their name, falling into Mississippi on the west side | 2,000 |
| Alibamous, a tribe of the Creeks | 600 |
| *Ouanakins | 300 |
| *Chiakaneseou | 250 |
| *Machecous ...... } Unknown, unless the author has put | 800 |
| *Caouitas ........ } them for tribes of the Creeks | 700 |
| *Souikilas | 200 |
| Miamis, upon the river of that name, falling into Lake Erie. | 350 |
| Delawares (les Loups) on the Ohio | 600 |
| Shawanese on Sioto | 500 |
| Kickapoos | 300 |
| Ouachtanons ..... } on the Ouabache | 400 |
| Peanquichas | 250 |
| Kaskasquias, or Illinois in general, on the Illinois river | 600 |
| *Pianris | 800 |
| Catawbas, on the frontiers of North-Carolina | 150 |
| Cherokees, behind South-Carolina | 2,500 |
| Chickasaws | 750 |
| Natchez .......... } Mobile and Mississippi | 150 |
| Chactaws | 4,500 |
|  | 56,500 |

†They live to the northwest, and the French, when they first saw them, took them for Spaniards.

The above list consists chiefly of such Indians as the French were connected with in Canada and Louisiana. Wherever we knew the names by which the different nations are distinguished by the English, we have inserted them. but the orthography is yet very unsettled, and the several nations marked with an * asterism are unknown to us, and therefore they are left as they stand in the original list.

So large a number of fighting men may startle us at first sight; but the account seems nowhere exaggerated, excepting only that the Catawba nation is now almost extinct. In some nations which we are acquainted with, the account falls even short of their numbers; and some others do not appear to be mentioned at all, or at least not by any name known to us.

Such, for instance, are the Lower Creeks, of whom we have a list according to their towns. In this list their warriors or gunsmen are 1180, and their inhabitants about 6000. Thus, a comparative judgement may be formed of the nations above-mentioned; the number of whose inhabitants will (in this proportion to their warriors, *viz*. 5 to 1) be about 283,000.

## ALSO FROM LEONAUR
### AVAILABLE IN SOFTCOVER OR HARDCOVER WITH DUST JACKET

**A HISTORY OF THE FRENCH & INDIAN WAR** *by Arthur G. Bradley*—The Seven Years War as it was fought in the New World has always fascinated students of military history—here is the story of that confrontation.

**WASHINGTON'S EARLY CAMPAIGNS** *by James Hadden*—The French Post Expedition, Great Meadows and Braddock's Defeat—including Braddock's Orderly Books.

**BOUQUET & THE OHIO INDIAN WAR** *by Cyrus Cort & William Smith*—Two Accounts of the Campaigns of 1763-1764: Bouquet's Campaigns by Cyrus Cort & The History of Bouquet's Expeditions by William Smith.

**NARRATIVES OF THE FRENCH & INDIAN WAR: 2** *by David Holden, Samuel Jenks, Lemuel Lyon, Mary Cochrane Rogers & Henry T. Blake*—Contains The Diary of Sergeant David Holden, Captain Samuel Jenks' Journal, The Journal of Lemuel Lyon, Journal of a French Officer at the Siege of Quebec, A Battle Fought on Snowshoes & The Battle of Lake George.

**NARRATIVES OF THE FRENCH & INDIAN WAR** *by Brown, Eastburn, Hawks & Putnam*—Ranger Brown's Narrative, The Adventures of Robert Eastburn, The Journal of Rufus Putnam—Provincial Infantry & Orderly Book and Journal of Major John Hawks on the Ticonderoga-Crown Point Campaign.

**THE 7TH (QUEEN'S OWN) HUSSARS: Volume 1—1688-1792** *by C. R. B. Barrett*—As Dragoons During the Flanders Campaign, War of the Austrian Succession and the Seven Years War.

**INDIA'S FREE LANCES** *by H. G. Keene*—European Mercenary Commanders in Hindustan 1770-1820.

**THE BENGAL EUROPEAN REGIMENT** *by P. R. Innes*—An Elite Regiment of the Honourable East India Company 1756-1858.

**MUSKET & TOMAHAWK** *by Francis Parkman*—A Military History of the French & Indian War, 1753-1760.

**THE BLACK WATCH AT TICONDEROGA** *by Frederick B. Richards*—Campaigns in the French & Indian War.

**QUEEN'S RANGERS** *by Frederick B. Richards*—John Simcoe and his Rangers During the Revolutionary War for America.

AVAILABLE ONLINE AT **www.leonaur.com**
AND FROM ALL GOOD BOOK STORES

# ALSO FROM LEONAUR
### AVAILABLE IN SOFTCOVER OR HARDCOVER WITH DUST JACKET

**JOURNALS OF ROBERT ROGERS OF THE RANGERS** by *Robert Rogers*—The exploits of Rogers & the Rangers in his own words during 1755-1761 in the French & Indian War.

**GALLOPING GUNS** by *James Young*—The Experiences of an Officer of the Bengal Horse Artillery During the Second Maratha War 1804-1805.

**GORDON** by *Demetrius Charles Boulger*—The Career of Gordon of Khartoum.

**THE BATTLE OF NEW ORLEANS** by *Zachary F. Smith*—The final major engagement of the War of 1812.

**THE TWO WARS OF MRS DUBERLY** by *Frances Isabella Duberly*—An Intrepid Victorian Lady's Experience of the Crimea and Indian Mutiny.

**WITH THE GUARDS' BRIGADE DURING THE BOER WAR** by *Edward P. Lowry*—On Campaign from Bloemfontein to Koomati Poort and Back.

**THE REBELLIOUS DUCHESS** by *Paul F. S. Dermoncourt*—The Adventures of the Duchess of Berri and Her Attempt to Overthrow French Monarchy.

**MEN OF THE MUTINY** by *John Tulloch Nash & Henry Metcalfe*—Two Accounts of the Great Indian Mutiny of 1857: Fighting with the Bengal Yeomanry Cavalry & Private Metcalfe at Lucknow.

**CAMPAIGN IN THE CRIMEA** by *George Shuldham Peard*—The Recollections of an Officer of the 20th Regiment of Foot.

**WITHIN SEBASTOPOL** by *K. Hodasevich*—A Narrative of the Campaign in the Crimea, and of the Events of the Siege.

**WITH THE CAVALRY TO AFGHANISTAN** by *William Taylor*—The Experiences of a Trooper of H. M. 4th Light Dragoons During the First Afghan War.

**THE CAWNPORE MAN** by *Mowbray Thompson*—A First Hand Account of the Siege and Massacre During the Indian Mutiny By One of Four Survivors.

**BRIGADE COMMANDER: AFGHANISTAN** by *Henry Brooke*—The Journal of the Commander of the 2nd Infantry Brigade, Kandahar Field Force During the Second Afghan War.

**BANCROFT OF THE BENGAL HORSE ARTILLERY** by *N. W. Bancroft*—An Account of the First Sikh War 1845-1846.

AVAILABLE ONLINE AT **www.leonaur.com**
AND FROM ALL GOOD BOOK STORES

## ALSO FROM LEONAUR
### AVAILABLE IN SOFTCOVER OR HARDCOVER WITH DUST JACKET

**AFGHANISTAN: THE BELEAGUERED BRIGADE** by G. R. Gleig—An Account of Sale's Brigade During the First Afghan War.

**IN THE RANKS OF THE C. I. V** by Erskine Childers—With the City Imperial Volunteer Battery (Honourable Artillery Company) in the Second Boer War.

**THE BENGAL NATIVE ARMY** by F. G. Cardew—An Invaluable Reference Resource.

**THE 7TH (QUEEN'S OWN) HUSSARS: Volume 4**—1688-1914 by C. R. B. Barrett—Uniforms, Equipment, Weapons, Traditions, the Services of Notable Officers and Men & the Appendices to All Volumes—Volume 4: 1688-1914.

**THE SWORD OF THE CROWN** by Eric W. Sheppard—A History of the British Army to 1914.

**THE 7TH (QUEEN'S OWN) HUSSARS: Volume 3—1818-1914** by C. R. B. Barrett—On Campaign During the Canadian Rebellion, the Indian Mutiny, the Sudan, Matabeleland, Mashonaland and the Boer War Volume 3: 1818-1914.

**THE KHARTOUM CAMPAIGN** by Bennet Burleigh—A Special Correspondent's View of the Reconquest of the Sudan by British and Egyptian Forces under Kitchener—1898.

**EL PUCHERO** by Richard McSherry—The Letters of a Surgeon of Volunteers During Scott's Campaign of the American-Mexican War 1847-1848.

**RIFLEMAN SAHIB** by E. Maude—The Recollections of an Officer of the Bombay Rifles During the Southern Mahratta Campaign, Second Sikh War, Persian Campaign and Indian Mutiny.

**THE KING'S HUSSAR** by Edwin Mole—The Recollections of a 14th (King's) Hussar During the Victorian Era.

**JOHN COMPANY'S CAVALRYMAN** by William Johnson—The Experiences of a British Soldier in the Crimea, the Persian Campaign and the Indian Mutiny.

**COLENSO & DURNFORD'S ZULU WAR** by Frances E. Colenso & Edward Durnford—The first and possibly the most important history of the Zulu War.

**U. S. DRAGOON** by Samuel E. Chamberlain—Experiences in the Mexican War 1846-48 and on the South Western Frontier.

AVAILABLE ONLINE AT www.leonaur.com
AND FROM ALL GOOD BOOK STORES

## ALSO FROM LEONAUR
### AVAILABLE IN SOFTCOVER OR HARDCOVER WITH DUST JACKET

**THE 2ND MAORI WAR: 1860-1861** *by Robert Carey*—The Second Maori War, or First Taranaki War, one more bloody instalment of the conflicts between European settlers and the indigenous Maori people.

**A JOURNAL OF THE SECOND SIKH WAR** *by Daniel A. Sandford*—The Experiences of an Ensign of the 2nd Bengal European Regiment During the Campaign in the Punjab, India, 1848-49.

**THE LIGHT INFANTRY OFFICER** *by John H. Cooke*—The Experiences of an Officer of the 43rd Light Infantry in America During the War of 1812.

**BUSHVELDT CARBINEERS** *by George Witton*—The War Against the Boers in South Africa and the 'Breaker' Morant Incident.

**LAKE'S CAMPAIGNS IN INDIA** *by Hugh Pearse*—The Second Anglo Maratha War, 1803-1807.

**BRITAIN IN AFGHANISTAN 1: THE FIRST AFGHAN WAR 1839-42** *by Archibald Forbes*—From invasion to destruction-a British military disaster.

**BRITAIN IN AFGHANISTAN 2: THE SECOND AFGHAN WAR 1878-80** *by Archibald Forbes*—This is the history of the Second Afghan War-another episode of British military history typified by savagery, massacre, siege and battles.

**UP AMONG THE PANDIES** *by Vivian Dering Majendie*—Experiences of a British Officer on Campaign During the Indian Mutiny, 1857-1858.

**MUTINY: 1857** *by James Humphries*—Authentic Voices from the Indian Mutiny-First Hand Accounts of Battles, Sieges and Personal Hardships.

**BLOW THE BUGLE, DRAW THE SWORD** *by W. H. G. Kingston*—The Wars, Campaigns, Regiments and Soldiers of the British & Indian Armies During the Victorian Era, 1839-1898.

**WAR BEYOND THE DRAGON PAGODA** *by Major J. J. Snodgrass*—A Personal Narrative of the First Anglo-Burmese War 1824 - 1826.

**THE HERO OF ALIWAL** *by James Humphries*—The Campaigns of Sir Harry Smith in India, 1843-1846, During the Gwalior War & the First Sikh War.

**ALL FOR A SHILLING A DAY** *by Donald F. Featherstone*—The story of H.M. 16th, the Queen's Lancers During the first Sikh War 1845-1846.

AVAILABLE ONLINE AT **www.leonaur.com**
AND FROM ALL GOOD BOOK STORES

## ALSO FROM LEONAUR
### AVAILABLE IN SOFTCOVER OR HARDCOVER WITH DUST JACKET

**THE FALL OF THE MOGHUL EMPIRE OF HINDUSTAN** by H. G. Keene—By the beginning of the nineteenth century, as British and Indian armies under Lake and Wellesley dominated the scene, a little over half a century of conflict brought the Moghul Empire to its knees.

**LADY SALE'S AFGHANISTAN** by Florentia Sale—An Indomitable Victorian Lady's Account of the Retreat from Kabul During the First Afghan War.

**THE CAMPAIGN OF MAGENTA AND SOLFERINO 1859** by Harold Carmichael Wylly—The Decisive Conflict for the Unification of Italy.

**FRENCH'S CAVALRY CAMPAIGN** by J. G. Maydon—A Special Correspondent's View of British Army Mounted Troops During the Boer War.

**CAVALRY AT WATERLOO** by Sir Evelyn Wood—British Mounted Troops During the Campaign of 1815.

**THE SUBALTERN** by George Robert Gleig—The Experiences of an Officer of the 85th Light Infantry During the Peninsular War.

**NAPOLEON AT BAY, 1814** by F. Loraine Petre—The Campaigns to the Fall of the First Empire.

**NAPOLEON AND THE CAMPAIGN OF 1806** by Colonel Vachée—The Napoleonic Method of Organisation and Command to the Battles of Jena & Auerstädt.

**THE COMPLETE ADVENTURES IN THE CONNAUGHT RANGERS** by William Grattan—The 88th Regiment during the Napoleonic Wars by a Serving Officer.

**BUGLER AND OFFICER OF THE RIFLES** by William Green & Harry Smith—With the 95th (Rifles) during the Peninsular & Waterloo Campaigns of the Napoleonic Wars.

**NAPOLEONIC WAR STORIES** by Sir Arthur Quiller-Couch—Tales of soldiers, spies, battles & sieges from the Peninsular & Waterloo campaigns.

**CAPTAIN OF THE 95TH (RIFLES)** by Jonathan Leach—An officer of Wellington's sharpshooters during the Peninsular, South of France and Waterloo campaigns of the Napoleonic wars.

**RIFLEMAN COSTELLO** by Edward Costello—The adventures of a soldier of the 95th (Rifles) in the Peninsular & Waterloo Campaigns of the Napoleonic wars.

## ALSO FROM LEONAUR
### AVAILABLE IN SOFTCOVER OR HARDCOVER WITH DUST JACKET

**AT THEM WITH THE BAYONET** by *Donald F. Featherstone*—The first Anglo-Sikh War 1845-1846.

**STEPHEN CRANE'S BATTLES** by *Stephen Crane*—Nine Decisive Battles Recounted by the Author of 'The Red Badge of Courage'.

**THE GURKHA WAR** by *H. T. Prinsep*—The Anglo-Nepalese Conflict in North East India 1814-1816.

**FIRE & BLOOD** by *G. R. Gleig*—The burning of Washington & the battle of New Orleans, 1814, through the eyes of a young British soldier.

**SOUND ADVANCE!** by *Joseph Anderson*—Experiences of an officer of HM 50th regiment in Australia, Burma & the Gwalior war.

**THE CAMPAIGN OF THE INDUS** by *Thomas Holdsworth*—Experiences of a British Officer of the 2nd (Queen's Royal) Regiment in the Campaign to Place Shah Shuja on the Throne of Afghanistan 1838 - 1840.

**WITH THE MADRAS EUROPEAN REGIMENT IN BURMA** by *John Butler*—The Experiences of an Officer of the Honourable East India Company's Army During the First Anglo-Burmese War 1824 - 1826.

**IN ZULULAND WITH THE BRITISH ARMY** by *Charles L. Norris-Newman*—The Anglo-Zulu war of 1879 through the first-hand experiences of a special correspondent.

**BESIEGED IN LUCKNOW** by *Martin Richard Gubbins*—The first Anglo-Sikh War 1845-1846.

**A TIGER ON HORSEBACK** by *L. March Phillips*—The Experiences of a Trooper & Officer of Rimington's Guides - The Tigers - during the Anglo-Boer war 1899 - 1902.

**SEPOYS, SIEGE & STORM** by *Charles John Griffiths*—The Experiences of a young officer of H.M.'s 61st Regiment at Ferozepore, Delhi ridge and at the fall of Delhi during the Indian mutiny 1857.

**CAMPAIGNING IN ZULULAND** by *W. E. Montague*—Experiences on campaign during the Zulu war of 1879 with the 94th Regiment.

**THE STORY OF THE GUIDES** by *G.J. Younghusband*—The Exploits of the Soldiers of the famous Indian Army Regiment from the northwest frontier 1847 - 1900.

### AVAILABLE ONLINE AT www.leonaur.com
### AND FROM ALL GOOD BOOK STORES

## ALSO FROM LEONAUR
### AVAILABLE IN SOFTCOVER OR HARDCOVER WITH DUST JACKET

**ZULU:1879** *by D.C.F. Moodie & the Leonaur Editors*—The Anglo-Zulu War of 1879 from contemporary sources: First Hand Accounts, Interviews, Dispatches, Official Documents & Newspaper Reports.

**THE RED DRAGOON** *by W.J. Adams*—With the 7th Dragoon Guards in the Cape of Good Hope against the Boers & the Kaffir tribes during the 'war of the axe' 1843-48'.

**THE RECOLLECTIONS OF SKINNER OF SKINNER'S HORSE** *by James Skinner*—James Skinner and his 'Yellow Boys' Irregular cavalry in the wars of India between the British, Mahratta, Rajput, Mogul, Sikh & Pindarree Forces.

**A CAVALRY OFFICER DURING THE SEPOY REVOLT** *by A. R. D. Mackenzie*—Experiences with the 3rd Bengal Light Cavalry, the Guides and Sikh Irregular Cavalry from the outbreak to Delhi and Lucknow.

**A NORFOLK SOLDIER IN THE FIRST SIKH WAR** *by J W Baldwin*—Experiences of a private of H.M. 9th Regiment of Foot in the battles for the Punjab, India 1845-6.

**TOMMY ATKINS' WAR STORIES: 14 FIRST HAND ACCOUNTS**—Fourteen first hand accounts from the ranks of the British Army during Queen Victoria's Empire.

**THE WATERLOO LETTERS** *by H. T. Siborne*—Accounts of the Battle by British Officers for its Foremost Historian.

**NEY: GENERAL OF CAVALRY VOLUME 1—1769-1799** *by Antoine Bulos*—The Early Career of a Marshal of the First Empire.

**NEY: MARSHAL OF FRANCE VOLUME 2—1799-1805** *by Antoine Bulos*—The Early Career of a Marshal of the First Empire.

**AIDE-DE-CAMP TO NAPOLEON** *by Philippe-Paul de Ségur*—For anyone interested in the Napoleonic Wars this book, written by one who was intimate with the strategies and machinations of the Emperor, will be essential reading.

**TWILIGHT OF EMPIRE** *by Sir Thomas Ussher & Sir George Cockburn*—Two accounts of Napoleon's Journeys in Exile to Elba and St. Helena: Narrative of Events by Sir Thomas Ussher & Napoleon's Last Voyage: Extract of a diary by Sir George Cockburn.

**PRIVATE WHEELER** *by William Wheeler*—The letters of a soldier of the 51st Light Infantry during the Peninsular War & at Waterloo.

AVAILABLE ONLINE AT **www.leonaur.com**
AND FROM ALL GOOD BOOK STORES

# ALSO FROM LEONAUR
## AVAILABLE IN SOFTCOVER OR HARDCOVER WITH DUST JACKET

**OFFICERS & GENTLEMEN** *by Peter Hawker & William Graham*—Two Accounts of British Officers During the Peninsula War: Officer of Light Dragoons by Peter Hawker & Campaign in Portugal and Spain by William Graham.

**THE WALCHEREN EXPEDITION** *by Anonymous*—The Experiences of a British Officer of the 81st Regt. During the Campaign in the Low Countries of 1809.

**LADIES OF WATERLOO** *by Charlotte A. Eaton, Magdalene de Lancey & Juana Smith*—The Experiences of Three Women During the Campaign of 1815: Waterloo Days by Charlotte A. Eaton, A Week at Waterloo by Magdalene de Lancey & Juana's Story by Juana Smith.

**JOURNAL OF AN OFFICER IN THE KING'S GERMAN LEGION** *by John Frederick Hering*—Recollections of Campaigning During the Napoleonic Wars.

**JOURNAL OF AN ARMY SURGEON IN THE PENINSULAR WAR** *by Charles Boutflower*—The Recollections of a British Army Medical Man on Campaign During the Napoleonic Wars.

**ON CAMPAIGN WITH MOORE AND WELLINGTON** *by Anthony Hamilton*—The Experiences of a Soldier of the 43rd Regiment During the Peninsular War.

**THE ROAD TO AUSTERLITZ** *by R. G. Burton*—Napoleon's Campaign of 1805.

**SOLDIERS OF NAPOLEON** *by A. J. Doisy De Villargennes & Arthur Chuquet*—The Experiences of the Men of the French First Empire: Under the Eagles by A. J. Doisy De Villargennes & Voices of 1812 by Arthur Chuquet.

**INVASION OF FRANCE, 1814** *by F. W. O. Maycock*—The Final Battles of the Napoleonic First Empire.

**LEIPZIG—A CONFLICT OF TITANS** *by Frederic Shoberl*—A Personal Experience of the 'Battle of the Nations' During the Napoleonic Wars, October 14th-19th, 1813.

**SLASHERS** *by Charles Cadell*—The Campaigns of the 28th Regiment of Foot During the Napoleonic Wars by a Serving Officer.

**BATTLE IMPERIAL** *by Charles William Vane*—The Campaigns in Germany & France for the Defeat of Napoleon 1813-1814.

**SWIFT & BOLD** *by Gibbes Rigaud*—The 60th Rifles During the Peninsula War.

AVAILABLE ONLINE AT **www.leonaur.com**
AND FROM ALL GOOD BOOK STORES

## ALSO FROM LEONAUR
### AVAILABLE IN SOFTCOVER OR HARDCOVER WITH DUST JACKET

**ADVENTURES OF A YOUNG RIFLEMAN** *by Johann Christian Maempel*—The Experiences of a Saxon in the French & British Armies During the Napoleonic Wars.

**THE HUSSAR** *by Norbert Landsheit & G. R. Gleig*—A German Cavalryman in British Service Throughout the Napoleonic Wars.

**RECOLLECTIONS OF THE PENINSULA** *by Moyle Sherer*—An Officer of the 34th Regiment of Foot—'The Cumberland Gentlemen'—on Campaign Against Napoleon's French Army in Spain.

**MARINE OF REVOLUTION & CONSULATE** *by Moreau de Jonnès*—The Recollections of a French Soldier of the Revolutionary Wars 1791-1804.

**GENTLEMEN IN RED** *by John Dobbs & Robert Knowles*—Two Accounts of British Infantry Officers During the Peninsular War Recollections of an Old 52nd Man by John Dobbs An Officer of Fusiliers by Robert Knowles.

**CORPORAL BROWN'S CAMPAIGNS IN THE LOW COUNTRIES** *by Robert Brown*—Recollections of a Coldstream Guard in the Early Campaigns Against Revolutionary France 1793-1795.

**THE 7TH (QUEENS OWN) HUSSARS: Volume 2—1793-1815** *by C. R. B. Barrett*—During the Campaigns in the Low Countries & the Peninsula and Waterloo Campaigns of the Napoleonic Wars. Volume 2: 1793-1815.

**THE MARENGO CAMPAIGN 1800** *by Herbert H. Sargent*—The Victory that Completed the Austrian Defeat in Italy.

**DONALDSON OF THE 94TH—SCOTS BRIGADE** *by Joseph Donaldson*—The Recollections of a Soldier During the Peninsula & South of France Campaigns of the Napoleonic Wars.

**A CONSCRIPT FOR EMPIRE** *by Philippe as told to Johann Christian Maempel*—The Experiences of a Young German Conscript During the Napoleonic Wars.

**JOURNAL OF THE CAMPAIGN OF 1815** *by Alexander Cavalié Mercer*—The Experiences of an Officer of the Royal Horse Artillery During the Waterloo Campaign.

**NAPOLEON'S CAMPAIGNS IN POLAND 1806-7** *by Robert Wilson*—The campaign in Poland from the Russian side of the conflict.

AVAILABLE ONLINE AT **www.leonaur.com**
AND FROM ALL GOOD BOOK STORES

## ALSO FROM LEONAUR
### AVAILABLE IN SOFTCOVER OR HARDCOVER WITH DUST JACKET

**OMPTEDA OF THE KING'S GERMAN LEGION** by *Christian von Ompteda*—A Hanoverian Officer on Campaign Against Napoleon.

**LIEUTENANT SIMMONS OF THE 95TH (RIFLES)** by *George Simmons*—Recollections of the Peninsula, South of France & Waterloo Campaigns of the Napoleonic Wars.

**A HORSEMAN FOR THE EMPEROR** by *Jean Baptiste Gazzola*—A Cavalryman of Napoleon's Army on Campaign Throughout the Napoleonic Wars.

**SERGEANT LAWRENCE** by *William Lawrence*—With the 40th Regt. of Foot in South America, the Peninsular War & at Waterloo.

**CAMPAIGNS WITH THE FIELD TRAIN** by *Richard D. Henegan*—Experiences of a British Officer During the Peninsula and Waterloo Campaigns of the Napoleonic Wars.

**CAVALRY SURGEON** by *S. D. Broughton*—On Campaign Against Napoleon in the Peninsula & South of France During the Napoleonic Wars 1812-1814.

**MEN OF THE RIFLES** by *Thomas Knight, Henry Curling & Jonathan Leach*—The Reminiscences of Thomas Knight of the 95th (Rifles) by Thomas Knight, Henry Curling's Anecdotes by Henry Curling & The Field Services of the Rifle Brigade from its Formation to Waterloo by Jonathan Leach.

**THE ULM CAMPAIGN 1805** by *F. N. Maude*—Napoleon and the Defeat of the Austrian Army During the 'War of the Third Coalition'.

**SOLDIERING WITH THE 'DIVISION'** by *Thomas Garrety*—The Military Experiences of an Infantryman of the 43rd Regiment During the Napoleonic Wars.

**SERGEANT MORRIS OF THE 73RD FOOT** by *Thomas Morris*—The Experiences of a British Infantryman During the Napoleonic Wars-Including Campaigns in Germany and at Waterloo.

**A VOICE FROM WATERLOO** by *Edward Cotton*—The Personal Experiences of a British Cavalryman Who Became a Battlefield Guide and Authority on the Campaign of 1815.

**NAPOLEON AND HIS MARSHALS** by *J. T. Headley*—The Men of the First Empire.

www.ingramcontent.com/pod-product-compliance
Lightning Source LLC
Chambersburg PA
CBHW031624160426
43196CB00006B/274